JACK OVER THE YEARS I HAVE SEEN YOUR LEADERSHIP ON TWO FRONTS. WHEN I HAD YOU AS A BASKETBALL PLAYER AND AS ONE OF MY FASTEST XC RUNNER EVER AT HAVEN MIDDLE SCHOOL. GOD HAS TRULY BLESSED ME WITH YOUR PRESENCE AND THE MANY MOMENTS WE HAVE SHARED ALONG THE WAY.

IT'S NOT A COINCIDENCE THAT YOUR CAREER DESIRE IS TO DESIGN, CREATE AND BUILD HUGE MONUMENTS. JACK, YOUR TRULY, BUILDING A STRONG FOUNDATION ON YOUR WAY TO "GREATNESS."

MUCH LOVE,

COACH JONES

2019

THE NEW
URBAN HOUSE

THE NEW URBAN HOUSE

A GLOBAL SURVEY

JONATHAN BELL AND
ELLIE STATHAKI

YALE UNIVERSITY PRESS

NORTH AMERICA

LATIN AMERICA

CONTENTS

EUROPE

AFRICA

ASIA

AUSTRALIA & NEW ZEALAND

INTRODUCTION

There are a vast array of parameters that can mold modern urban residential architecture. The varying conditions—social, cultural, economic, geographic, climatic—that shape cities around the world all bring different factors to bear on how the modern house is planned, designed, and built. Yet a house is not only an architectural statement, but also a social one, reflecting the tastes and desires of its owners, the economic circumstances that facilitate its creation, and, most intriguing of all, the way its designers and inhabitants choose to relate to the context around them.

This book is an exploration of the many design responses to the challenges posed by the modern city today and the ways in which architects from around the globe address the issues they encounter. As you might expect, the featured projects vary hugely, showcasing multiple approaches to the most common architectural challenge of all: the shaping of space for changing patterns of life.

Building in the modern city has become more and more of an architectural problem. The need to combine the logistical demands of contemporary life with increasingly high levels of environmental performance, along with the ever-changing urban context, ensures that the single-family city house will always be a true material, logistical, and technical jigsaw puzzle. Throw into the mix the inescapable budgetary restrictions that every project carries, each client's distinct set of requirements, and the intense and dynamic client–architect relationship that such a personal project inevitably brings, and the contemporary urban residential architect has a difficult task ahead. This book showcases architectural solutions as opportunities; from the most awkward plots and the most testing briefs often come the most exciting spatial solutions.

The house is the commonest typology in architecture, its function unchanged for millennia. What has evolved are our requirements, our needs, and the way we relate these to the world at large. What is the house's place in the modern city? From the twentieth century onward, the world has been defined by massively increased urbanization. In

2016, the United Nations estimated that 54.5 percent of the world's population lived in cities, a figure that was expected to grow to 60 percent by 2030. The rise of megacities—those with 10 million or more inhabitants—continues relentlessly, with the next ten megacities all expected to emerge from developing countries. Although cities are efficient, they still place massive demands on infrastructure, energy, and materials.

All these considerations have marginalized the private house; density, planning, pragmatism, and raw economics have become far more pressing concerns. Modern architecture was intended to improve the built environment, yet the story of the twentieth-century modernist house was defined by spectacular and unique one-off villas. Detached and isolated from other houses, these projects drew inspiration from site and nature, rather than from the proximity of others or the legacy of pre-existing typologies.

For vast swathes of urbanites, the single-family house is not only impractical, but also unattainable. This book acknowledges the huge range of different experiences around the world and their importance in creating a coherent narrative for the modern history of urban dwellings. Yet throughout the twentieth century and beyond, the single-family house also served as a test bed for innovation in materials, forms, planning, and density. Even when the seemingly uncompromising, gloriously abstract mansions of the pioneering modernists were placed in a dense, messy, and intense urban setting, they too had to adapt—softened and at the same time enriched by the bustling life around them.

Such is the power of the urban context. Pierre Chareau's Maison de Verre in Paris (1932), for example, primarily used steel and glass as an exercise in honesty in materials. At the same time, the facade's translucent glass blocks form a convenient external skin to filter light and views both inside and out, negotiating subtly the way the interior relates with the house's urban surroundings. Around the same time, Le Corbusier was also experimenting with building in compacted settings. Many of the architect's Parisian residential projects, such as the house and studio for the painter Amédée Ozenfant (1922), Villa Cook (1926) and the Maison Planeix (1928), were where he explored using his clean white geometric forms, contrasting them against the Parisian roofscapes, all the while developing his manifesto on the "Five Points of Architecture."

The city provided architects with a proving ground for their ideas, a place where norms could be challenged, techniques and materials explored, and planning and programs forensically dissected. Few clients are willing to submit themselves to such uncertainties, which is why the most innovative modern urban houses are often those designed for architects for themselves. Maison de Verre was pioneering and unique, but over the past century there were countless other examples, such as Konstantin Melnikov's avant-garde house and studio in Moscow, completed in 1929, Brian Housden's family house in Hampstead (1965), and Richard Murphy's layered home in Edinburgh (2014). Indeed, the architect's own home could be all things: an evolving paean to concrete abstraction, a singular structure that was essentially a work of art in it own right, or a treasure trove of space-saving ideas, mechanisms, and interlocking spaces.

And while the experiments continued, the twenty-first century brought rather more pressing challenges. Demand for space in cities the world over is higher than ever and new buildings must meet stringent energy-saving requirements, while a thicket of planning regulations, particularly in historic urban centers, have to be negotiated. At the same time, in an era when the impact of global, over-arching architectural manifestos, such as the International Style, is weakening, variety and a multiplicity of voices and regional approaches have become the name of the game. In short, there is no one way to design a modern urban house.

This book presents a survey of these many different architectural solutions, typologies, and approaches. However, even within this level of diversity, common trends and coherent narratives begin to emerge on an international level. Space is at a premium in most global urban hubs, forcing architects and planners to explore what "compact" living truly means, both in terms of well-being and raw economics. Meanwhile, rapid urbanization in the twentieth and twenty-first centuries led to high levels of pollution in many developing global metropoles. An eco-friendly approach is now more critical than ever before.

The best contemporary urban architecture suggests that invention and innovation are increasingly important. Pragmatism and expertise come together to explore new ways of building in the city, regardless of location. This book presents a variety of solutions, within environments that range from suburban to urban, ancient to modern. The most universal quality is privacy, and the desire to improve our engagement with our urban surroundings while also seeking separation and distance. It must also be said that wealth and privilege play an enormous role in shaping contemporary architecture, as has always been the case.

To complicate things even further, the definition of "urban" varies, too. Featured contexts range from closely packed narrow buildings in small winding streets and clusters of historical edifices, to the airiness and grandeur of Parisian boulevards. Sites in the heart of town play an equally crucial role in the city-living experience as the periphery's generous and planted suburban lots, and some cities' sprawl can go for miles, blending the suburban with the outright rural and making it hard to tell exactly where the city ends and nature begins. Unsurprisingly, the suburban residential complexes of Asia and South America feel a world away from the traditionally dense, cheek-by-jowl townhouses and the jigsaw-like urbanism of cities such as London and Los Angeles, where only innovation and ingenuity can bring architecture into compact sites. All these elements form different nuances of the urban experience.

Organized geographically, the book required extensive research into many different cultures, attitudes, and approaches. Every project provides a new insight into the conditions that shape the architecture of some of the world's major cities, through recent history, signature styles, and current conditions on the ground. The research laid bare the myriad challenges facing architects, whether they were addressing existing context and vernacular, trying to create defensive space, or simply dealing with the economics of urban construction. It brings together a huge variety of approaches, from the reinvention of long-standing vernacular forms such as terraces and townhouses, through to the fast-changing suburbs and inner cities of modern Japan, where the short lifespan of family houses provides architects with a laboratory for aesthetic and technical experimentation.

Regardless of scale and budget, this book is about celebrating architecture that enhances the experience of living in a city. Despite the unstoppable rise in city dwelling, it is clear that there will never be a universal experience of the metropolis. This is a guide to the ways that design can address increasingly pressing issues; it raises a toast to the endearing value of urban living and our engagement with the city itself.

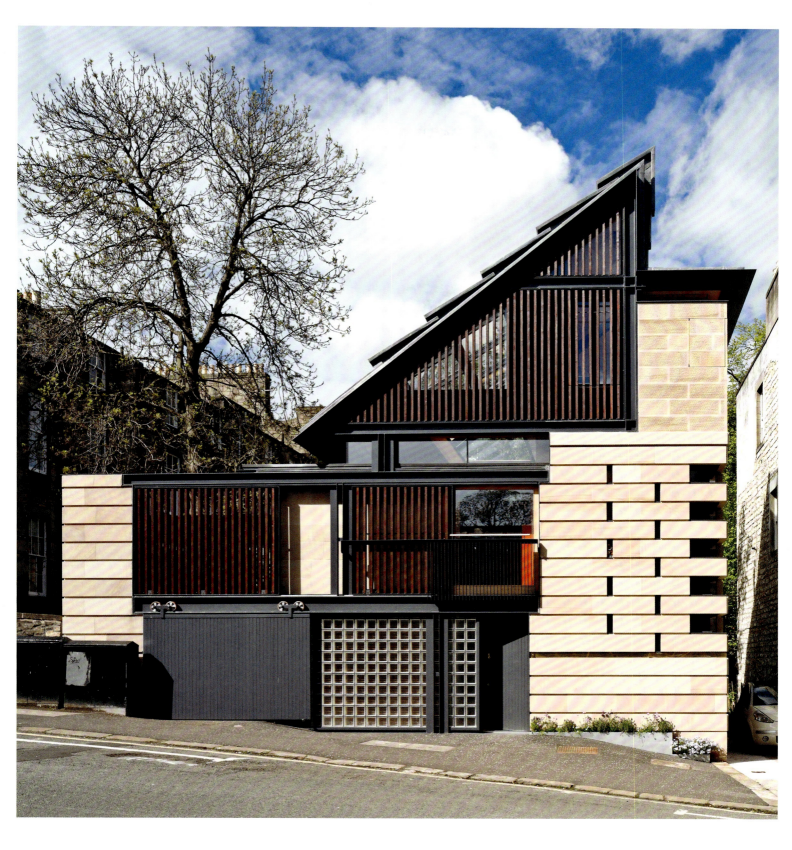

NORTH AMERICA

VANCOUVER TORONTO MONTREAL
SAN FRANCISCO OXNARD LOS ANGELES
HOUSTON CHICAGO NEW ORLEANS
SYRACUSE NEW YORK MIAMI BEACH

2 Levitt & Sons built only six types of houses in Levittown, PA. They were all single-family dwellings and the construction process was highly regimented. Building began in 1952 and was completed in 1958, during which time 17,311 homes were built.

Domestic architecture in North America compressed the evolution of millennia into a few hundred years, with imported colonial styles adapted to local conditions and materials. Indigenous architecture and culture had very little impact on the gradual takeover of the United States, serving as an exotic other that could easily be swept away by the "civilizing" virtues of known architectural styles and forms. North America soon evolved its own specific conditions, stylistic quirks, and regional traits, but it was only with the arrival of new technological developments—automobiles, air conditioning, elevators—that a distinctly American form of architecture emerged.

The United States is the place where modernism meets the demands of the market head on, and ideology and aesthetics are intertwined with commerce and fashion. It was here that the vision of the International Style reached its purest form, both in the curtain-walled office blocks of glass and steel that had stumbled in a Europe scrambled by war and in the elegant villas that brought the modernist dreams of light, transparency, and space to life in the perfect climate and culture. It was also a place where the social ethos of modernism—a movement that had its roots in egalitarianism and improving conditions at all stages of society—collided spectacularly with the possibilities of scale.

The new architecture proved itself more than adept at delivering spectacular forms, literal cinematic visions for a society raised on strong expressions of meritocracy and success. Yet whereas the most visible expressions of North American architecture came to dominate the cultural conversation, the everyday experience of housing was far more prosaic. The homogeneity of the American Dream showed a fundamental conservatism in approaches to domestic design. For every Levittown—the generic name given to the segregated suburbs built by the firm of Levitt & Sons and ultimately consisting of around 140,000 houses in New York, Pennsylvania, Maryland, and New Jersey—there were countless, often lesser imitators.

The United States was the land of the automobile, and consequently the land of the suburb. Driven by the postwar GI Bill, the housing legislation set in train to rehouse returning US soldiers, the new suburbs brought home ownership to a much greater swathe of society than ever before. And as consumer culture ramped up in the postwar era, the American Dream was increasingly distilled into a clichéd materialist checklist of house, car, refrigerator, backyard, and barbecue: the bounties of mass production and consumption distributed among society. However, the white picket fences and compact traditionally styled houses of the new suburbs concealed massive structural social inequality that consumption and design were ill-equipped to tackle.

In the United States, as elsewhere, the house's role as a place of experimentation and innovation has always been confined to the fortunate few, usually those at the very top of the market. Indeed, some of the examples in this book prove that privilege is usually the best place from which to make a statement of difference. However, architects are increasingly aware of their role within society, and as the gulf between rich and poor grows ever wider, there have been some notable attempts at democratizing the housing process. While New York's boroughs have rapidly gentrified and the hillsides of Los Angeles and San Francisco have ascended into the stratosphere of the 1 percent, cities such as Detroit, Houston, and New Orleans have seen the opposite, with falling populations, decaying housing stock, and a real pressing need for change.

Perversely, the United States is also the land of the McMansion, the all-you-can-eat buffet of domestic architecture, where styles and materials collide on a plate in an unapologetic display of taste and status. McMansions are typically dismissed as being ungainly hangovers of the worst excesses of vernacular symbolism, the unthinking offspring of, say, Frank Lloyd Wright's effortless synthesis of craft, scale, form, and tradition. Instead, we see columns and colonnades, four-car garages and facades free from proportion or scale. Arguably, there are also modernist McMansions, sprawling angular palaces that have little in

common with the ideals of the early modernists. They proliferate in communities such as Palm Springs and the Hamptons, once showcases of innovation and elegance, but also long-standing bastions of privilege.

Although the promise of the factory-built house was tantalizingly predicted by the likes of Le Corbusier, Jean Prouvé, and Buckminster Fuller, the prosaic reality has been the tens of thousands of prefabricated homes that are still churned out by North American factories. These range from single-width transportable units, designed for easy delivery, to bespoke vernacular creations indistinguishable from their hand-crafted siblings. The new-found status of contemporary design has caused a small but significant resurgence in the idea of a truly modernist machine-made home, but these remain decidedly niche; modern design is not, and never has been, a mass-market choice.

That said, the modern house—in particular the urban house— is more attuned to context than a neoclassical design delivered to site on the back of a flatbed truck. Mindful of the cost of tailoring designs to specific sites, young US architects are pioneering flexible designs that can be adapted for a variety of sites and contexts. Many US cities are so scattered that truly urban architecture has never really existed, and probably never will, but where economics permit, density is the next frontier of innovation. The suburb might still be the blueprint for an individual dream, but it is a poor use of increasingly precious resources, be they water, fuel, materials, or even time. Yet, even the modest urban houses that exploit overlooked sites by maximizing building codes and material innovation are just a drop in the ocean, the preserve of a fortunate few with the time and skills to take advantage of these rare opportunities.

The American house will always be a symbol of status. Even though the country was a refuge for the ideals of the Bauhaus and some of the pioneers of the Modern Movement, the intersection with the insatiable demands of commerce saw US modernism take a journey of compromises and extremes. In an increasingly politically polarized country, housing issues are contentious but potentially unifying and beneficial to all. The template of modernism still has much to give.

ROUGH HOUSE

This house is an architectural experiment, a rare case of a true collaboration between the architects that designed it and the craftspeople and tradespeople who worked on its detailing and ornamentation. Aiming to create a residence out of a true democratic process, Vancouver-based firm Measured Architecture approached this commission for a single family house on a narrow urban plot from an unusual angle; instead of designing everything and handing over their wish list to specialists, who would then work to bring their visions to life, they rooted their design in the "handmade" right from the get-go.

The team focused on a meaningful collaboration with the building teams, landscape designers, artisans, and tradespeople who worked on the house's design and construction. The building that emerged is the Rough House. Working with recycled materials and green building systems and processes, as well as maintaining a constant dialogue with all the people at all levels of the scheme and the surrounding context, the architects created a project for which each and every person involved feels a fulfilling sense of ownership.

The house's minimalist, yet warm and tactile aesthetic is achieved through a carbonized cypress exterior cladding, board-form concrete, and whitewashed timber boards. Natural wood and painted surfaces inside create the necessary accents for a playful and homely interior. A central staircase wrapped in weathering steel plate acts as a border and transitional space, dividing the house into two parts: the single-story west side and the two-level garden-side volume.

The building spans three levels. The basement houses the generous master bedroom suite, with en suite bathroom and walk-in wardrobe. This level also holds amenities such as a laundry room and wine cellar, as well as a guest bedroom. The ground level is the house's main living space, including living, kitchen, and dining areas, a separate informal family room and support areas. This floor opens up

1 The house's warm and tactile aesthetic was achieved using recycled materials.   2 Rough House is rooted in handmade design and bespoke craft.   3 Large floor-to-ceiling openings merge the interior of the house with the lush garden outside.

to a decked terrace that merges effortlessly with the indoors via large floor-to-ceiling openings. The top floor is dedicated to the family's children, featuring their two bedrooms, a playroom, and access to a green roof.

The architects were careful to frame views of nature through the house's several windows of varied sizes. This meant that the laneway studio on the edge of the plot was given a living wall and green roof. This sense of being connected with nature was further enhanced in the house by sustainability features that were "quietly woven into the project," explain the architects, thereby allowing this humble home to achieve a significant energy efficiency rating.

4 A lower ground level features the master bedroom suite.
5 Views out from the main living space reveal the studio and living wall. 6 Architects, artisans, and tradespeople collaborated on the immaculate detailing of Rough House.

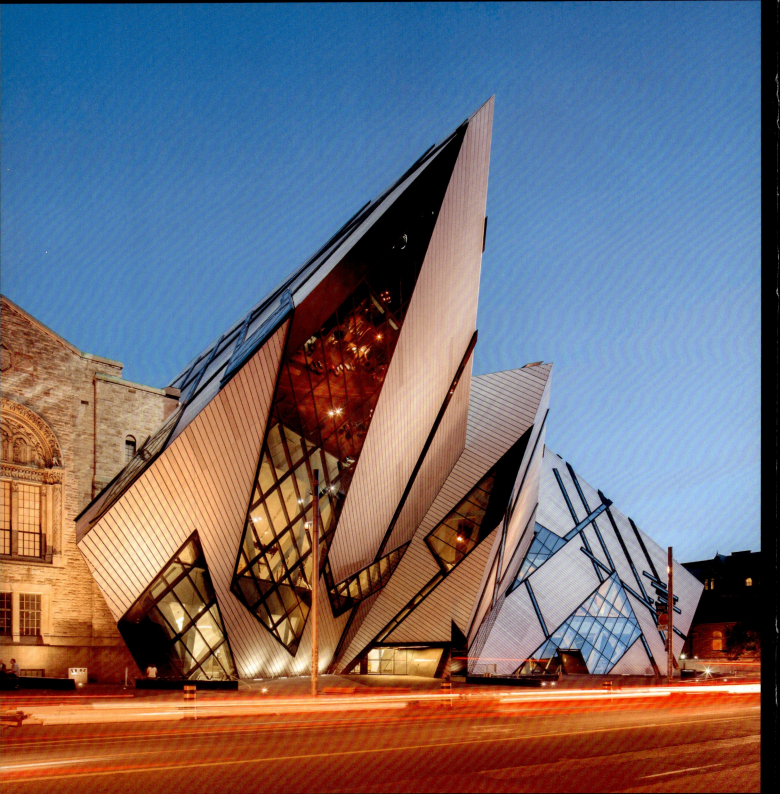

TORONTO

1 The Lee-Chin Crystal at Royal Ontario Museum was designed by Studio Daniel Libeskind. It has been admired for the innovation and engineering complexity involved in the self-supporting prismatic structures.   2 The beautifully detailed houses located in The Annex neighborhood were mostly built between 1880 and the early 1900s. Typically, Annex houses are made of red brick.

Canada's largest city is not especially well known for the character of its residential architecture. From its origins as a series of indigenous villages through to its role as a trading post, the growing city was only named Toronto in 1834. Today, it claims to be one of the world's most diverse cities, a focal point for many waves of immigration throughout the eighteenth, nineteenth, and twentieth centuries. Appropriately enough—and perhaps because of its rich mix of cultures—Toronto also has an eclectic range of architectural styles, from the towering downtown that makes it one of the high-rise capitals of the northern hemisphere to the extensive suburbs only a few blocks away, laid out in classic grid style. The city marches along the Lake Ontario waterfront, gradually downscaling into a wide variety of residential areas of different periods and styles.

From the middle of the nineteenth century, the railway added another level of complexity and also lines of demarcation. As a result, modern Toronto is arranged as a number of explicitly zoned areas, from the entertainment district through to the commercial zone, university neighborhood, and a few surviving industrial areas. The elaborate Victorian magnificence of the Old City Hall stands in stark contrast to Brutalist icons such as the Ontario Science Centre and the space-age modernism of the New City Hall, with its twin curving towers, completed in 1965 to a design by the Finnish architects Viljo Revell, Heikki Castrén, Bengt Lundsten, and Seppo Valjus. Like many large cities, Toronto suffered from radical demolition and reconstruction during the postwar era, with big expressways doing their best to sweep away character and fine grain. As a major port, it also has a long history of diversity and mixed neighborhoods, with Chinatown, Greektown, Portugal Village, and Little India all featuring on the modern map.

Gentrification is reshaping the modern city. Major new developments such as Studio Daniel Libeskind's Royal Ontario Museum have had the requisite effect, increasing an interest in arts and culture and changing the perception of whole neighborhoods. The city even had an icon before the term became fashionable, in the form of Will Alsop's elevated faculty building at the Ontario College of Art and Design (OCAD), a pixelated box atop canted columns rendered in the architect's signature colors, mediating the change in scale between the high-rise core and the ranks of low-rise housing at the city's periphery. Frank Gehry also has plans for OCAD's campus, as part of the Mirvish+Gehry apartment complex that should see two of the country's tallest condo towers; the fact that the native Torontonian's name is attached to the development signifies the high esteem in which he is held in Canada.

is Canada's tallest residential building. It was designed by Graziani + Corazza and completed in 2014. **4** The present-day Chinatown is centered around Spadina Avenue and Dundas Street, after the first Chinatown was demolished to make way for Toronto City Hall.

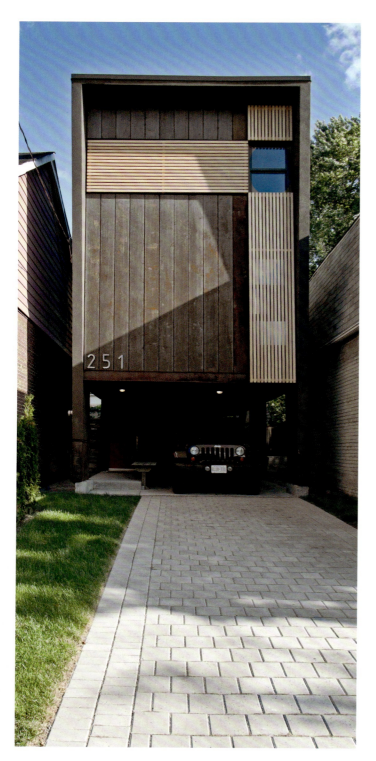

SHAFT HOUSE

Walking down this sleepy Toronto residential street, one cannot help but notice the new, tall, and narrow house that has been slotted between the area's existing older buildings. It is the work of locally based architect Reza Aliabadi, and the structure—rather fittingly known as Shaft House—is a modern exercise in architectural frugality.

The detached house spans two and a half stories, but sits in a plot that is only a modest 20 feet (6 m) wide. Budgetary restraints were a key driver in the project—they fueled Aliabadi's urge to search for a creative solution. He worked with sustainable and cost-efficient materials, such as aluminum siding, untreated wood, and recyclable rusted steel, to compose a house that looks and feels thoroughly contemporary. What's more, its steel cladding will slowly change color over time, thus giving the impression that the building is aging organically.

In terms of the house's internal arrangement, the clue is in the name. A void—a shaft—is cut through the center of the volume and brings natural light deep into the house. There is a distinct absence of walls inside; this helps sunlight to penetrate throughout, and also creates the impression of extra space. The structure's main circulation core and services are built around this void, which also cleverly acts as a space divider for the house's different functions. A shift in levels strengthens the same effect, helping to define various rooms. Living spaces are nestled in the house's middle levels, with a garage on the ground floor and a south-facing roof deck at the top. Bedrooms and bathroom are tucked away at the higher levels. A set of oversized steps on the lower floor leads out toward the back and the house's garden.

Shaft House is a small but perfectly formed bespoke home; it is also a paradigm of efficiency in urban residential design, demonstrating that being affordable does not mean a piece of architecture cannot be innovative or fun.

1 Shaft House is a contemporary addition to Toronto's housing stock.   2 The garden is accessed via oversized steps.   3 Inside, the house is arranged around a central void.   4 The staircase circulates around the central shaft.

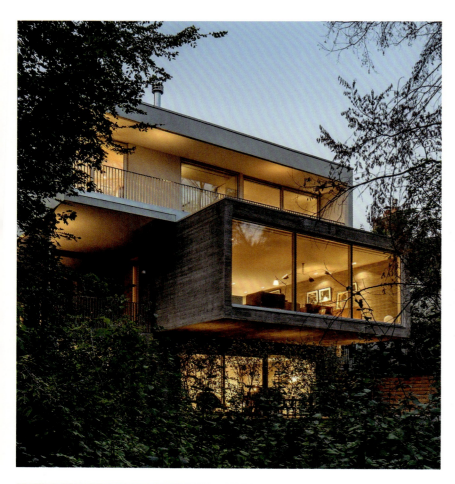

TORONTO

COUNTRY Canada
ARCHITECT Angela Tsementzis YEAR 2015

CONCRETE HOUSE

Building within an urban context does not have to mean sacrificing all hope of living next to nature, as Canadian architect Angela Tsementzis and her Concrete House clients have proved. When a couple of branding professionals approached Toronto-based Tsementzis to design their dream home in a ravine in the city's Moore Park district, staying in touch with nature was high on their list of priorities; equally important was to create a house that would reflect their minimalist aesthetic. The architect obliged, on both fronts.

Concrete House is perched on a tree-filled slope, and although it is only a short drive from the city center, it can rival the best of rural holiday homes. Following her clients' brief, Tsementzis placed the verdant surroundings at center stage, thus ensuring that nothing else—decorative or otherwise—steals the spotlight, in any part of the house. The structure is composed of three simple stacked volumes in concrete and bright white plaster. Large expanses of glazing frame the greenery, bringing the outside in. The poured *in situ* concrete is matched by oak wood, travertine stone, and white plaster touches inside, thereby making for a fairly restrained and sophisticated material palette.

The most prominent middle volume contains the heart of the house: the living, dining, and kitchen areas, arranged in an open-plan setting, perfect for entertaining as per the clients' request. Jutting out of the composition some 15 feet (4.5 m) toward the ravine, it makes for a perfect hangout for partying among the trees. The semi-sunken volume below houses a more informal sitting area—the family room—while the home's three bedrooms are nestled at the structure's top. Plenty of outside areas, such as terraces on the higher levels and a garden on the ground floor, ensure that the residents can not only look at the trees around them from within, but also truly connect with nature, thus making the most of this remarkable house's leafy location.

1 This Toronto home is located in a ravine. 2 Concrete and wood contribute to the minimalist aesthetic. 3 Large glazed openings bring the leafy outside in. 4 Lots of outdoor areas encourage interaction with nature.

1 At the rear of the house, a large steel-clad
volume overhangs the garden. 2 The windows
on the first floor are carefully positioned to frame
views of the treetops.

1
2

DULWICH RESIDENCE

The Dulwich Residence transforms a suburban structure into a sleek modern dwelling, with the judicious use of contemporary materials and radically reworked massing and internal volumes. Located in the Montreal suburb of Saint-Lambert, the structure began life as a brick-built house from the 1920s. The clients, a young family, required an extension and internal reconfiguration to meet their needs. The original house's rather boxy and four-square design stood in stark contrast to the more traditional pitched roofs and detailing of its close neighbors, but also gave Montreal architects naturehumaine the opportunity to graft on an extension with a bold new aesthetic.

The architects have effectively added 50 percent more space, mostly through the creation of a new block that is joined to the front facade of the original house by a slim glazed volume, giving it a standalone presence. Despite having a total floor area of around 2,845 square feet (264 sq m), there was still space to create three separate double-height areas, linking the public ground floor with the more private set of rooms upstairs. A contrasting contemporary brick was used in juxtaposition with the original red brick, and the new-built element is set back and subservient to the original front facade, which has a restored raised porch.

At the rear of the house these roles are reversed, with the plain brick form of the original house set against a new, robustly detailed wooden terrace and the glazing of the new addition. The materials are also bolder, with faceted steel cladding to the first floor, raised up above brick piers. This part of the new addition contains another double-height volume and what the architects describe as a "sleeping basket," a small place of refuge with striking views of the forested site, set alongside a home office space. Interior finishes include wooden cladding, industrial balustrades, and stone and wood floors. A master bedroom with en suite bathroom occupies the rest of the

new extension, with a stairwell placed in the slot between old and new. On the ground floor, the existing walls were removed to create an open-plan living space, with the double-height kitchen/dining area overlooking the garden. Rows of pendant lights emphasize the verticality of the space, while a built-in dining table mirrors the form of the new fenestration. Finally, a playroom was created in the new half-basement, with a small sunken courtyard bringing in light and views to the garden. The architect's sensitive handling of an original structure has resulted in a new house that acknowledges its past without being beholden to heritage.

3 The dark wood contrasts with the light interior decoration.
4 The open-plan kitchen is located in the old section of the house.   5 The architect chose the white steel mesh balustrade "for its geometric effect and the transparency it provides."

SAN FRANCISCO

San Francisco is renowned for its rolling hills, 1950s tram line, Golden Gate suspension bridge, and the liberal and creative attitude of its inhabitants. It is also known for its beautiful and pricey housing stock, which ranges from Victorian townhouses—bay windows are one of the city's architectural characteristics—to twentieth-century and contemporary styles. Following a couple of decades of a booming economy, a thriving local tech industry, and an ever more confident art scene, today San Francisco finds itself ranking pretty highly in the world's livability ratings, which makes it the perfect breeding ground for striking new housing.

The city's distinct geography, set on the tip of a peninsula, surrounded by water and small islands and dotted with hills, provides a natural landscape that is rich and varied. This creates a diverse setting, which has led to a wide selection of different housing solutions, as well as a range of architectural challenges. A mild climate year round is counterbalanced by San Francisco's notorious cool winds and fog, a result of the distinct topography.

In fact, the many hills and valleys often create their own specific microclimate, leading to what effectively is one city that has many different weather reports. For a local architect in San Francisco, variety is the name of the game. Change and diversity have, however, been among the city's key characteristics historically. Today's San Francisco is the result of the rapid growth of the city's suburbs in the mid twentieth century, and the "Manhattanization" of downtown areas later on in the 1970s and 1980s. This was the era that brought one of the city's most iconic constructions, the Transamerica Pyramid by William Pereira & Associates, which opened in 1972. And while several earthquakes have caused untold destruction to this beautiful seaside town, its residents' tenacity has meant that it has kept being rebuilt—and, every time, improved.

This should come as no surprise, as San Francisco is a city that has been fueled by hope and ambition for centuries. Just as the late nineteenth century's gold rush attracted many of its later permanent—and often, wealthy—inhabitants, today's tech industry

cene, ever since the dot-com revolution started in the 1990s, followed by the social media boom of the noughties. Today, tech giants such as Apple and Google have the Silicon Valley as their main base, revitalizing nearby San Francisco as a result. Not that Silicon Valley money has been the only currency flowing into the city: new attitudes and businesses across town, such as a thriving gallery scene, have also been changing the social and creative landscape of late—for better or worse.

The city first capitalized on its wealth of historic buildings in the 1970s and 1980s, with rapid gentrification driven by the tech booms that have echoed around the Valley right up to the present day. As a result, urban housing can be ruinously expensive, although talk about the housing market bubble bursting has recently been gathering pace. This would be the second housing spike and bubble of the twenty-first century for this fast-growing North American urban hub. However, it has not stopped local architecture practices such as Jensen Architects, Ogrydziak Prillinger Architects, Schwartz and Architecture, and IwamotoScott from designing numerous contemporary townhouses, which range from new builds to bold renovations of existing housing. These now make up San Francisco's modern housing stock, which draws inspiration from global trends and reflects the well-traveled and sophisticated tastes of its creators and owners. Historical conversions with sleek, new open-plan floor plans and modern backyard extensions are a common typology, accounting for a large chunk of the city's family dwellings. This might soon change, though, as several high-profile architects, including Jeanne Gang and OMA, have been putting proposals through for high-rise condominium towers, taking luxury living to the vertical.

Cultural offerings have been respectively increasing in variety, to follow the diverse and moneyed crowd's demands. They include the by-all-accounts successful expansion of Mario Botta's SFMoma by Snøhetta, and, at the opposite side of the bay, the Berkeley Art Museum and Pacific Film Archive, recently completed by one of the art scene's favorite architecture practices, Diller Scofidio + Renfro. What bankers and stock brokers are to the evolution of New York's lofts, tech entrepreneurs are to San Francisco's thriving arts and architecture scene.

Back on the residential front, there is evidence that technology and architecture can evolve hand in hand in San Francisco. It would feel only natural that a city with such smart residents would have some pretty intelligent housing to match. Swiss-born industrial designer and entrepreneur Yves Béhar and art consultant Sabrina Buell's home in San Francisco's hip Cow Hollow neighborhood is a case in point. Possibly one of the city's most high-tech homes at the time of its completion, it is the epitome of a contemporary marriage between residential architecture and the digital world: services non

1 San Francisco is known for its hilly terrain and iconic rows of Victorian townhouses. 2 The Transamerica Pyramid tower opened in 1972 and remains the city's tallest skyscraper.

up to the push of a button, the front door locks and unlocks automatically—if it knows you, that is—and light and temperature are naturally computer-controlled to perfection. This environment would indeed make sense for the founder of Fuseproject, a company that so far has pioneered everything from low-cost computers for developing countries to an ultra-sleek, wireless and compact speaker. Elsewhere in the city, other tech-led projects are following suit.

Even if the housing market slows down, this little pocket of the world is where at least part of the future happens and, as such, San Francisco has a lot to offer to the architecture scene. And the residential front can only benefit from the association. Multidisciplinary collaborations, cross-disciplinary projects, and an insatiable appetite for the new and the "now" that spills over to the art and the architecture scene make this North American city one of the most exciting ones to watch.

SAN FRANCISCO
COUNTRY USA
ARCHITECT Ogrydziak Prillinger **YEAR** 2009

1 Open-plan living spaces that look out to the
San Francisco skyline form a key part of this home.
2 Gallery House features a distinctive metal
lattice on its front facade.

GALLERY HOUSE

Dense urban environments, socioeconomic changes, and conflicting needs often give birth to new typologies and buildings of a hybrid function, such as New York's live/work lofts and the traditional scenario of living above the shop in Asia's shophouses. Architects Zoë Prillinger and Luke Ogrydziak, and their clients, took this concept one step further with a West Coast commission in 2009 called Gallery House.

Built in San Francisco's South Park borders, this project had a brief that called not only for a home for a pair of passionate collectors, but also a semi-private gallery space within the same building, where the couple could display their art. The combination was intended to allow the clients—a virologist and a mathematician who exclusively collect work by female contemporary artists—to enjoy and share their findings with the world, and at the same time redefine the idea of living with art. This is a new domestic typology, a "gallery house,"

where the presence of art is felt everywhere but its role ranges in intensity throughout and transforms in response to different room functions.

In Ogrydziak Prillinger's design, the gallery and the domestic wings merge with open-plan arrangements and areas that are dedicated to displaying art spread across all parts of the building. The composition was conceived as a sequence of interlocking volumes, "identified as solid or void," explain the architects. The facade's expressive metal mesh lattice was imagined as an abstract representation of the area's bay windows, and is a playful interpretation of the local planning regulations. It also acts as a light veil, symbolically protecting the glass-enclosed interiors behind it. The architects cleverly placed a sawtooth roof over the main circulation stairwell, which floods the interior with north light—the ideal type for viewing art in the rooms underneath.

The gallery is situated on the ground level, easily accessible from the street, to cater for opening parties, artist and curator talks, and events, as well as the practical requirements of moving large art pieces. Above it sit two floors of residential use. Large openings bring the outdoors in on all levels, yet at the same time operable walls and heated floors are incorporated to create a sense of protection from San Francisco's varied weather.

A terrace crowns the top. Ogrydziak Prillinger filled this green roof, which also serves as the gallery's sculpture garden, with drought-resistant plants. This level has been pierced with skylights, which help daylight to stream deep inside the rooms below.

3 The project's residential areas are located on the two upper floors.   4 The ground level hosts the gallery, which the owners use to share their private collection with the world.   5 A roof terrace on the structure's top floor.

1 Telegraph Hill House is elevated above the city.
2 The open-plan living room and kitchen occupy the top floor.

TELEGRAPH HILL HOUSE

Telegraph Hill House takes full advantage of its location, integrated with San Francisco's topography to provide incredible city views. Designed by Feldman Architecture, the project involved the comprehensive overhaul of an existing building that lacked even a certain period charm, with a plain facade and a narrow compartmentalized interior. The architects' aim was to open up the new house to city views, maximizing the living space both horizontally and vertically. Consequently, the house plan was inverted to make the most of the vistas. The ground floor is given over to parking and servicing (as well as a San Francisco staple, the yoga room), with a bedroom, family room, and den located on the second floor, three more bedrooms (including the master) on the third floor and an impressive open-plan living area on the top floor. A partly glazed rear deck offers up classic skyline views, and features a built-in barbecue and planters.

Today, the original house is completely unrecognizable. The old facade has been entirely reinvented with gray limestone cladding and new metal window frames, giving the building a crisp, contemporary appearance. The new top story is designed to read as an independent penthouse, raised up above the city. In this respect, it almost feels like a self-contained apartment, high up atop a condominium. The other innovative use of space is vertical, with circulation catered for by a new bespoke wood, steel, and glass staircase. A section of structural glass flooring in the top-floor living area brings light down to the landing below.

The open-plan kitchen, living room, and deck read as one area, practically inviting the surrounding cityscape—with its undulating waves of housing and signature skyscrapers—into the room. Outdoor space is at a premium in hilly San Francisco, and Telegraph Hill House makes the most of a top-floor deck by including an external staircase

that winds its way up from the entry level. Another small terrace can be accessed from the kitchen, making the most of the house's dual aspect. A slender steel pergola continues the rhythm of the glazing out onto the top-floor terrace.

Privacy was a key driver behind Feldman Architecture's design, but as with almost all of San Francisco's housing stock, Telegraph Hill House cannot help but be a player on a much wider stage. The views out and across the city's hilltops are as integral to the interior experience as the sequences of living space, thereby creating a house that feels immersed within the city.

3 Reflective surfaces and inset glass floors bring light to the lower levels.   4 The spectacular view from the main terrace takes in Saints Peter and Paul Church and the towers of Russian Hill.

VAULT HOUSE

Beach-side houses in this part of Southern California typically follow the traditional "shotgun" style, which involves a long and narrow structure that delineates its plot and has entrances on both ends of the site. Los Angeles-based architects Sharon Johnston and Mark Lee decided to give the genre a twist by creating a house in Oxnard that has its roots in the shotgun typology but is thoroughly modern, with a strong sculptural quality.

The result is Vault House, an expressive dwelling set on a densely developed strip of beach about a ninety-minute drive north of Los Angeles. Composed as a series of unidirectional rooms spread across two floors, the house clearly stands out among its neighbors, cut through using a repeated vault pattern that appears on doors, skylights, windows, and openings throughout. An open courtyard at the center of the structure breaks up the sequence of rooms and brings in light, which subtly moves through the space during the course of the day creating a soft shadow play. The courtyard also acts as a sheltered main entrance hall, offering a modern alternative to the traditional shotgun house double-entrance setting.

Perched lightly on the sand, Vault House is lifted on pylons so that it can survive swells of the sea and tsunamis, in accordance with the restrictions outlined by the California Coastal Commission. While the residence looks as if it is made of sculptural concrete, it is in fact built using plaster and a wood frame—a decision that the architects made after they discovered that timber helps the house better withstand the area's frequent earthquakes.

Inside, the main floor includes an open-plan living, kitchen, and dining area, orientated toward the sea. A series of more private secondary rooms—a study and guest suites—is on the same level, but placed toward the rear of the house. The top floor simply holds the master bedroom, with its roomy bathroom and walk-in wardrobe.

1 Curves and arches give the house its sculptural feel.
2 Orientated toward the sea, the open-plan living room is lifted on pylons.   3 The house's top level comprises the master bedroom, which appears filled with light.

4 A courtyard in the building's heart highlights the main entrance.   5 Windows and nooks were designed carefully to display the owners' art collection.

A garage slots underneath the top floor, toward the back. All three levels are connected by a single staircase, reaching up to an accessible roof terrace where residents can enjoy long vistas.

The numerous arches that pepper the design not only define the Vault House's geometric character and inspire its name, but are also cleverly placed to direct the visitor's gaze, expertly framing the owners' art collection and the house's other key feature—the striking ocean views.

6 The Vault House's long, narrow structure references
Southern California's shotgun house typology.

6

EEL'S NEST HOUSE

The American suburban experience has traditionally been one of untrammeled space. Occasionally, however, growth is geographically confined, leading to an atypical level of density. Los Angeles is usually defined as a city built on sprawl and the liberating potential of the automobile. This new-build house is located in one of the city's most crowded neighborhoods, Echo Park, an area boxed in by freeways and bisected by Sunset Boulevard.

Replacing a 1929 building on an extremely modest plot, the new house occupies the bulk of the site. Anonymous Architects received permission to add an extra story, doubling the built area allowed without giving up the garage (an essential component of Los Angeles car culture), and an outdoor space in the form of a roof terrace. "The name 'Eel's Nest' is often given to very narrow lots in Japan," says Simon Storey of Anonymous. The plot width in Echo Park is just 15 feet (4.5 m); despite these limitations, the end result is a two-bedroom, one-bathroom house of 960 square feet (89 sq m).

Set on a corner with multiple aspects and vistas, Eel's Nest has a generous roof terrace, from where the view takes in the Hollywood sign and the San Gabriel Mountains, despite the urbanized hills that surround it. Above the single-car garage is a living/dining space running the full length of the lot. The second floor contains two bedrooms arranged around a central bathroom, and the upper floor is a decked terrace with planters and roof lights, with a private grove of olive trees creating what the architect describes as an "elevated garden." Wooden flooring is paired throughout with built-in cabinets, while the stairway also helps bring light all the way down into the plan. Anonymous Architects used a rough-edged modernism that keeps visual distractions to a minimum, with the fire-proofing placed on the external walls due to the house being built right up to the property line. To make the most of the light and the views down the street, the first and second floors have huge facades of glass.

1 The kitchen, living, and dining spaces open out onto the courtyard garden.   2 The fully decked and planted roof terrace creates a little oasis.   3 The house sits atop a garage, thereby eking living space from an unpromising site.

SHOTGUN CHAMELEON

The Shotgun Chameleon house derives its name from a familiar piece of vernacular design. The "shotgun" style refers to a modest, usually single-story residence arranged as a linear series of interconnected rooms (one alleged origin of the name is linked to the idea that a shotgun could be fired from the front door to the back, straight through the open rooms). Originating in the American South in the nineteenth century, shotgun houses became associated with low-income urban areas and offered many advantages, from the low build cost through to the natural ventilation in the hot southern climate.

Shotgun Chameleon is in Freedmen's Town, Houston's historic Fourth Ward. The passively ventilated house is set back from the street but uses a slatted wooden skin to provide privacy to the exterior balconies and porches, socially important features that characterize the area's domestic architecture. In less domestic environments, this "chameleon-like" front screen could be shaped to reorient the ventilation or even to serve as a billboard or commercial frontage. Shotgun Chameleon has two bedrooms on the ground level, alongside a covered porch, and a further bedroom and open-plan living/dining area on the double-height first floor. The roof pitch slopes backward from the street to the rear of the property, and the raised-up main living space finishes with a wall of glass and a balcony accessed by sliding glass doors. Throughout the year, the space can be ventilated naturally, with windows angled to soak up low winter sun and avoid the high summer heat. Low-e glass, lots of insulation, and renewably sourced wooden cladding and fittings give the house a low energy footprint. The floor plan is also flexible: close the internal stair and the single house model is converted into an up-and-down duplex, with the upstairs unit accessed by the external stair. It also lends itself to commercial use, mindful of the shifting patterns of occupation that continue to impact on the United States' urban landscape.

1 The interchangeable front screen allows the design to be adapted to different urban contexts.   2 The side yard leads to the main entrance.   3 Flexible spaces are created by opening sliding doors.

CUT TRIPLEX TOWNHOUSE

The townhouse needs to be an incredibly flexible typology. Quite aside from local conditions and materials, it has to be able to adapt to its site, invariably a unique setting that requires architectural ingenuity to preserve privacy and light. The Cut Triplex Townhouse is located in Chicago's East Village. Spacecutter Architects were tasked with creating a balance between "privacy and openness," with a long, narrow site flanking a small, south-facing alley. Light is brought into the interior via a 59-foot (18 m) ribbon of shaded windows at first-floor height, sitting atop a monolithic brick pedestal that anchors the house to the ground. At each end of the building, fully glazed walls admit light to the ground-floor reception areas, with more conventional window openings punctuating the upper floors. Black manganese brick gives the house a subtly modulated dark form.

Inside, white walls and wooden floors are paired with black ribbon steel detailing and tiling. Bold splashes of color in the children's bathroom and on the main staircase—painted Yves Klein Blue—are juxtaposed with the monochrome finish in rooms such as the kitchen. Two floors of reception and family rooms are topped with a four-bedroom upper floor and a roof terrace that offers spectacular downtown views. Another bedroom and media room are located on the lower ground floor. Light wells are set into the front and rear of the property, effectively "detaching" the interior from the monumental brick shell that provides security and privacy.

In some respects, the house is classically formal, with the raised first floor given over to entertaining spaces, including a music room and a living room. The kitchen and dining areas are on the second floor, with two staircases providing alternative routes through the space. The contrast between solid external walls (up to 18 inches/ 45 cm thick in places) and deep concrete foundations (Chicago has soft lakebed soil) and light-filled interior spaces with red oak floors and long strips of glass gives the Cut Triplex a unique character.

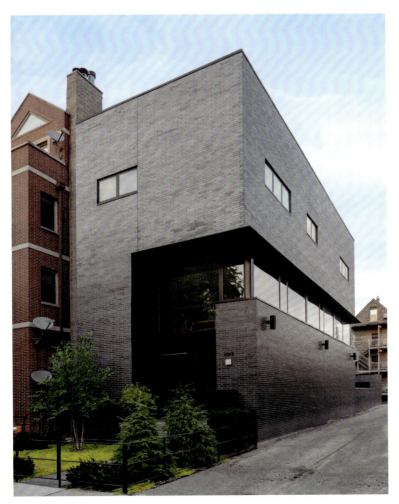

1 A long window creates a cinematic view of the neighborhood.
2 The main living room has sliding doors onto the rear terrace.   3 The strip window is set deep in the black brick facade.   4 Cut Triplex makes an imposing corner statement.

3106 ST. THOMAS

The contemporary American South has been an unwitting proving ground for new housing typologies. Ravaged by consecutive economic downturns and major natural disasters, such as Hurricane Katrina in 2005, the region has an understandably strong demand for affordable urban housing. The Office of Jonathan Tate is one of several studios working on developing low-cost housing based on the surfeit of vacant plots in cities such as New Orleans. This approach to creating flexible housing design is counter-intuitive in most housing markets, but enticing investment and residents into unused spaces and demolished lots is a ground-up way of improving the local economy. Jonathan Tate calls this approach the "Starter Home* thesis," and he has written extensively on the dominance of the house ownership model in the United States and how it might evolve. For example, how might a new generation benefit from the stability and investment provided by real estate without having to conform to the debased values that shape the current model?

The house at 3106 St. Thomas in New Orleans is a practical application of Tate's thinking. Described as a "speculative infill single-family house," the slender structure occupies a narrow plot in the city's Irish Channel neighborhood, a district of generally low-density and often historic housing. "A Starter Home* expects no *tabula rasa*, and in fact relies on the specificities of site in order to function at its best, financially, urbanistically, and spatially," Tate writes. With all these qualities thrown into the pot on an undersized site, the architect and his studio are to be commended for creating an eccentrically shaped dwelling that responds to its mixed neighborhood, with adjacent warehouse and housing.

The house is distinguished by the twin peaks of its roof lines, the tallest reaching a generous height of 40 feet (12 m). The result is a zigzag profile that runs the length of the site, creating a complex section of double-height spaces, angled ceilings, and mezzanines.

1   2

1 This is a narrow site, with high ceilings that make the most of the limited space. The corner window provides a view of the street.   2 Low-cost metal siding and roofing give the house a uniform industrial appearance.

Inside, finishes and fittings are deliberately kept simple. An open-plan ground floor makes the most of the bulk of the floor area, while bedrooms and bathrooms are tucked into the upstairs eaves, beneath the jagged roofscape.

In many respects, the house at 3106 St Thomas has much in common with Japanese residential design, with its narrow site and modest scale, modulated by monolithic metal cladding and quirky profile. In the United States, however, real-estate conditions are markedly different, with the housing itself adding value to the land, rather than the other way around.

3 Close proximity to the neighboring building allows for plenty of glazing without fear of being overlooked. 4 A slim deck wraps around the structure. 5 Detailing inside and out is industrial grade and hard wearing.

HAFFENDEN HOUSE

Inspired by architect and artist Gianni Pettena's Ice House from 1972—an art piece in which Pettena encased a whole suburban house in Minnesota within a giant ice cube—Haffenden House is the work of Jon Lott, a Design Critic in Architecture at Harvard's Graduate School of Design and founder of the PARA Project architecture practice.

In fact, despite its name, Haffenden House is technically not a house at all. Created within a quiet residential street in Syracuse, and in the architectural vernacular of a dwelling, this is a private writing studio and retreat for a poet. However, it was designed to suggest a home, seeking to address the notion of the generic suburban residence. Lott opted to work with a "nuanced void," playing with ideas of sameness and looking to inject an element of surprise into the sleepy street. "I wanted to reference the Ice House, as a blank spot within the repetitive image of house," explains the architect.

The unusual structure spans three levels and includes a garage on the ground floor; an open-plan writing space on the first, which is lined floor to ceiling with bookshelves and includes a minimalist bathtub, theatrically dug into the floor plate by the window; and a reading room on the top level. The owner's actual home is next door, and the writing studio is delicately connected to it on the first floor. From the outside, though, Haffenden House reads as a completely autonomous structure. The front exterior is made of bright white plaster, peppered with small openings. At the rear, sheets of translucent silicon-impregnated fabric—material traditionally used for roofs and canopies—cover the large glazed facade like a curtain, protecting the user's privacy when needed. A curved wall contrasts the structure's clean orthogonal exterior and divides the first and second floors, "maximizing indirect light for the second level and avoiding any association with the landscape on the third," continues Lott. This curve makes the reading room "softer," thereby allowing the residents to fully immerse themselves in their literary undertaking.

1 The exterior view of the house from the rear yard.
2 A large opening is protected by a sheet of translucent fabric.   3 Floor-to-ceiling bookshelves line the library space.
4 A bathtub is cut out from the sleek white floor.

NEW YORK

New York is a city of extreme architectural contrasts. As the global nexus—if not the original birthplace (which was Chicago)—of the steel-framed skyscraper, the city inspired architectural awe and envy throughout the twentieth century with its impressive and very physical manifestation of wealth, drama, and financial might. With the turn of the century, decline and blight culminated in terror and disaster, bringing an unwelcome global focus on this most cosmopolitan of cities. Nevertheless, since the events of September 2001, New York has rebuilt itself in almost every conceivable way, from the thrusting new towers for the new generation of financial giants, to the grass-roots regeneration that pivots awkwardly between self-conscious gentrification and all-out, developer-led frenzy.

Few modern cities give so little clue as to the geology, geography, culture, and landscape of the original realm they occupy. Stand in Midtown Manhattan today, and it is impossible to believe that the sylvan, rolling spaces of Manna-hata—as the first colonialists deduced the island was called—are only five centuries in the past. For the Italians, French, Dutch, and British, Manhattan and its environs—at the mouth of the mighty Hudson River—offered a springboard for trade with the American interior, as well as a staging point for the Atlantic slave trade. As a new nation emerged out of internal and external strife, New York earned a reputation as a place of dissent and political fervor, becoming the United States' first capital city and ultimately the country's primary generator of not only physical trade but also commodities and stocks, culture and art, spreading across the five boroughs (Manhattan, the Bronx, Queens, Brooklyn, and Staten Island).

For the earliest residents, living in New York owed a great deal to the domestic style and preferences of the colonists' home countries, from the modest Dutch design of Wyckoff House (1652)—Brooklyn's oldest residence—to the classic brownstone of the Victorian era, a grand European townhouse reinvented for the generous streets of New York. The rigor of the Manhattan grid simply emphasized the city's scale. The influence of former lives also drove the creation of the city's mighty lung, Central Park, laid out in the European Romantic style by Frederick Law Olmsted from the 1850s onward. The 800-acre (324 ha) park swept away organic, chaotic growth and replaced it with an idealized version of landscape. Ironically, Central Park's own fortunes ebbed and flowed over the century, just as the city's impressive terraces of housing stock dropped in status, converted into multiple occupation, yet without losing their sense of grandeur.

There are few starker juxtapositions than the one between the hefty Fifth Avenue mansions of the proto-Masters of the Universe,

...ho ruled nineteenth century Wall Street, and the city's workers' tenements—and later the "projects," the public housing blocks built throughout the century. This social housing gave the huddled masses space and amenity standards that would once have been unthinkable in a city so devoted to the dog-eat-dog machinations that have always been the callous flip side of the American Dream. Yet, regardless of whether you are rich or poor, New York still soars deliriously, a world of towering objects that implies a future of change, innovation, and better things. It is the city of perpetual optimism.

In the early twentieth century, New York's image became synonymous with the rise of the skyscraper, with landmark projects such as the Empire State Building and the Chrysler Building dominating the skyline since the 1930s. These early architectural behemoths literally raced from the ground to their spires, and the vertiginous imagery of the skeletal steel city under construction still stands as a potent symbol of modernism. Elevators were also integral to this rush to the sky, with the Cooper Union's Foundation Building housing the world's first passenger elevator shaft, built in 1853. Burnham and Dinkelberg's well-known Flatiron Building, completed in 1902, also retained its original hydraulic lifts for more than a century.

New York's love affair with high rises never really ceased, and in more recent times a new wave of tall buildings has been taking the city by storm. Today, however, there is even more status and prestige in living high. The city that gave the world the penthouse apartment is trying to eclipse these ornate palaces in the sky with a new generation of supertall apartment buildings. The unspoken competition for the tallest, mightiest, most eye-catching superstructure is fierce. Rafael Viñoly's 432 Park Avenue was the world's tallest residential building upon its completion in 2015. More "starchitects" have been busy reaching for the stars: Herzog and de Meuron, Frank Gehry, Renzo Piano, Zaha Hadid, Richard Meier, BIG, and OMA have all worked on tall housing projects in the city.

New York's cultural hotspots are equally celebrated, with the Museum of Modern Art and the Metropolitan Museum leading the way. Frank Lloyd Wright's instantly recognizable Guggenheim Museum is one of the city's signature buildings, a sculpture for art. In terms of more recent additions, SANAA's New Museum helped put the now-acclaimed Japanese practice on the global architecture map, while openings such as the new Whitney Museum of American Art by Renzo Piano and the Met's big plans with David Chipperfield for a new wing mean the city's creative clout is steadily rising.

Until recently, non-locals would be forgiven for thinking of New York as mostly Manhattan. However, the rise in real-estate terms of the vast expanses of Brooklyn and key upcoming projects in Queens and New Jersey highlight the swathes of—mostly—residential areas and rolling suburbs that make up greater New York. They are dominated by housing in all its forms: there are overcrowded blocks of flats (an echo, perhaps, of those notorious nineteenth-century inner-city tenements); rows of iconic brownstone terraced houses; larger detached mansions in neo-Gothic and Victorian styles; and, more recently, modern residences, purpose built for the creative crowds that have the spending power to add their architectural mark to the city, but have been priced out of traditionally desirable Manhattan.

Gentrification is in full swing, reaching far and wide, with both private buyers and developers searching for more "affordable" areas to build on. Bushwick, Williamsburg, and Greenpoint, all in Brooklyn, are the new poster neighborhoods for the twenty-first-century hipster generation. Districts such as these have become a land of architectural experimentation, with designers trying out both modern styles and new technologies, including ones that favor sustainability and a more eco-friendly approach. At the same time, large chunks of land surrounding Manhattan are being redeveloped, such as Asbury Park in New Jersey (by architects such as Miami-based Chad Oppenheim) and the former Rheingold Brewery site in Bushwick (by ODA). They herald the reinvention of whole areas, which were often industrial and disused in their previous lives but have now become shorthand for the city's growing aspirations and prosperity.

4 Classic brownstones have seen changing fortunes over the decades. Currently, they are at the peak of their value and appreciation. 5 New York is a city of striking wealth, as the grand apartments and penthouses of Fifth Avenue and other well-known addresses testify.

SOUTH SLOPE TOWNHOUSE

South Park Slope is one of the frontiers of Brooklyn's relentless rush to gentrification. The jewel in the crown is the restored brownstone, the iconic stone-built townhouse, typically with steps leading up to a raised ground floor and with projecting bay windows. Etelamaki Architecture's South Slope Townhouse is cut from a different cloth, defiantly contemporary in material and form even as it conforms to the street pattern and scale of traditional development.

The house is actually a duplex above a ground-floor rental space, a radical reconstruction that uses the core of the original building for character and combines it with a modern facade of corrugated steel. Unlike many of the surrounding streets, with their well-regulated brownstone facades, this particular block was eclectic and varied, with buildings ranging from 1900s-era apartments through to contemporary condos. According to the architects, this "presented an opportunity for a bold facade design." Although the material used is rigorous and industrial, the windows are placed in such a way as to retain the general rhythm of the street, without compromising the overall composition of glass and galvanized metal cladding.

Inside, key features of the original structure are retained, such as the brick chimney breast that forms a focal point of the duplex living space and top-floor master bathroom. The space and light evoke the classic New York loft, with industrial-style metal balustrades and wooden flooring. The main living area is largely open plan, divided into two key sections (eating/living and a more secluded space for work and television). Bedrooms are on the top floor, with a generous master-bedroom suite taking up the front of the building.

Throughout the house, the architects used off-the-shelf materials and fixings, with custom elements deployed sparingly to create character and individuality. A world apart from the neighborhood's traditional architecture, the South Slope townhouse proves that contemporary design still has a place in the heart of historic Brooklyn.

1 Sliding doors maximize interior space.   2 The facade is a careful composition of textures and surfaces.   3 The living space overlooks the street.   4 The staircase has steel balustrades.   5 The master bedroom enjoys a quiet outlook.

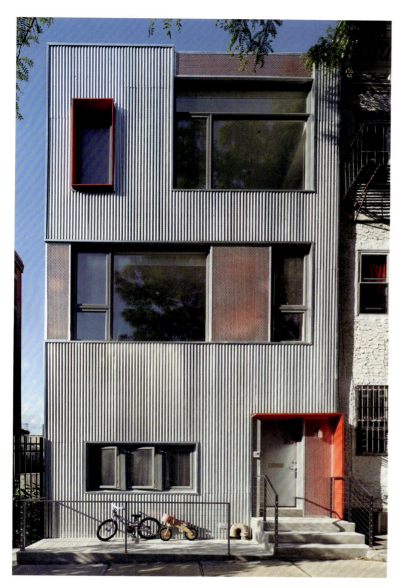

URBAN TOWNHOUSE

With the Urban Townhouse, architects GLUCK+ adapted the traditional New York residence to enhance its sense of retreat from the urban environment. Its presence is concealed behind a full-height metal screen, with a complex pattern shaped from water-cut aluminum. This urban veil shields a tall, narrow row house with an unconventional plan. To make the most of the site—and to preserve a sense of privacy—the architects placed the staircase at the very front of the plan in a location typically taken up by a parlour or front room.

GLUCK+ describes the approach as akin to that of "open loft living," but with the practicality of having a row house right on a New York street. Inside, the staircase winds around an elevator core, simultaneously serving as a spectacular vertical four-story library, a towering shelf stack that runs right through to the top of the house. The townhouse is characteristically narrow—38 feet (11.5 m) deep on a 70-foot (21 m) site—and the floors are treated as a series of independent, open-plan spaces, evoking the character and space of a traditional New York loft. The main living room occupies a mezzanine space above a double-height dining area, opening onto a small courtyard garden; there is also a roof terrace on the top floor. Glass floors and balustrades help bring light down the stairwell. The metal facade is perforated by a brick-inspired abstract pattern that allows even more light to filter in and out of the house. At dusk and after dark, it glows from within, supplemented by two thin strips of glazing on either side of the panel.

At the rear, the facade is all glass, filling the open-plan living spaces with light. A simple material palette of brick, stone, and wood is used throughout, even in the courtyard garden. The project was designed to accommodate a relatively low budget and was correspondingly straightforward to build. Slotted in-between two older buildings, it gives little clue as to the invigorating space within.

1 The plan includes a master suite that spans the fourth floor.
2 The main living room is on a mezzanine level.   3 Beneath it sits the kitchen and double-height dining room.   4 The metal facade is cut with a pattern inspired by the surrounding brick buildings.

MIAMI BEACH

COUNTRY USA

ARCHITECT Christian Wassmann   YEAR 2015

SUN PATH HOUSE

Designing houses within an urban context in many cases means tweaking or adding to existing buildings, often with unexpected results. New York-based architect Christian Wassmann's Sun Path House is a case in point. Created for chef and restaurateur Frank Prisinzano and his family, this is no ordinary house extension. The sculptural concrete structure (cast *in situ*) was designed to complement the owner's adjacent 1930s bungalow in Miami Beach, yet its curvaceous forms and hanging gardens sit in stark and playful contrast to the surroundings, creating a dialogue between old and new and redefining the client's "center of living."

When it comes to the architect's design inspiration, the clue is in the name of the house. Standing three stories high, Sun Path House takes its cue from the universe, as its orientation and the curves of its walls were precisely designed to follow the sun's path during the longest day of the year. While celebrating the celestial body and Miami's abundant sunshine and pleasant weather through the means of architecture, Wassmann also uses the sun "to foster vitality and health in its inhabitants."

An extensive kitchen and outdoor dining area on the ground level spatially link the old house with the new wing. The composition's curved spine pierces through the extension, at the same time "structural, functional, and sculptural,"points out Wassmann. It encloses a chimney and a wood-fired pizza oven, and also houses the structure's main circulation core—a staircase gently encouraging the visitor to climb up. The client's brief mentioned a "treehouse," and while the sturdy Sun Path House may not be a stereotypical version, it is the genre's concrete equivalent, with its hanging vine gardens, narrow base and cantilevered top volumes. One floor above ground, the curve unfolds into a master bedroom with a round bed and a 360-degree aspect, as well as a bathroom and a small study area.

1 A small study on the main living level of the extension overlooks the garden.   2 Warm timber contrasts the rough concrete inside.   3 Sun Path House's striking structure is an elegant extension to an existing 1930s bungalow.

4 A decked terrace makes a perfect sun trap.   5 The glazed living space is wrapped in a growing green screen.   6 The house's elegant curves were designed to follow the path of the sun during the longest day of the year.

Light streams in through the glass walls, filtered and protected by a curtain of hanging greenery that surrounds the square floor plan. Warm timber in floors, ceilings, and detailing balances the interior's rough concrete shell, giving it a warm, domestic feel.

The roof was also put to good use, transformed into a timber-lined sun deck for the residents. Surrounding it, a curved tall wall poetically—and fittingly—mirrors the path of the sun on the summer solstice, also protecting the user from winds and prying eyes. Sun Path House is an exercise in geometry, astronomy, and architecture, bringing together different disciplines in an unexpected, playful, and ultimately delightful whole.

LATIN AMERICA

MEXICO CITY SÃO PAULO CONCEPCIÓN
BUENOS AIRES LUQUE

The twenty nations of Latin America are now so diverse that it may be difficult to recall the time when it was conventional to dismiss the continent as a single homogeneous cultural block. Long-standing independence from colonial powers, hugely diverse populations, geographical variety, and frequently volatile economic conditions have all helped to shape the region's modern architecture in new and often invigorating ways. In many respects, the architecture of Latin America is dominated by the role of the continent's largest country, Brazil, the crucible of regional modernism. During the 1920s and 1930s, the fervent ideals of European modernism were beginning to cross the Atlantic, and it was in Brazil that they found the most fertile ground. However, Brazilian modernism had humble beginnings; between 1927 and 1928, the Ukrainian-born architect Gregori Warchavchik built the Casa Modernista in São Paulo, a boxy white-walled villa that would not look out of place in a British seaside resort. It was an inauspicious start to ninety years of innovation, with some of the most technically and structurally inventive explorations of modern forms and materials.

Renowned Swiss-French architect Le Corbusier visited Brazil as part of a pioneering lecture tour in 1929. By the mid 1930s, he had started a long-running collaboration with the Brazilian architect and urban planner Lúcio Costa; together they designed the Ministry of Education and Health Building in the Centro district of Rio de Janeiro. Costa eventually went on to study and work in New York with Oscar Niemeyer, and both architects ultimately became the driving force behind Brasília, the country's new capital city, founded in 1960. When Niemeyer died in 2012, at the age of 104, he left behind a substantial legacy of built work, creative collaborations, and inspiration. The whole continent was infused by his flowing, almost spiritual connection with the built environment.

Brazil led, but other countries were quick to follow. Paradoxically, Brazil's industrialization lagged behind that of some of its neighbors, especially Argentina, but state patronage and the alignment of architects with engineers saw the profession achieve high status. In 1948, the Faculty of Architecture and Urbanism was founded at the University of Buenos Aires, highlighting the transference of teaching ideas from Europe and the United States to Latin America. Architects such as Amancio Williams in Argentina and Niemeyer himself worked closely with industry, especially concrete manufacturers, exploring prefabrication and new methods of manufacture to help realize their visions.

In terms of climate, Latin America has distinct advantages over the extremes posed by the northern hemisphere. Modern architecture was emphatically about increasing and improving access to space and light, with these elements seen as an essential component of a socially motivated plan for improved living conditions. Extreme heat and humidity were not in the pattern book of Bauhaus-trained designers, and it was the architects of Latin America who were tasked with reinventing the materials, programs, and aesthetics of modernism for a very different world. Shading, screens, and a more refined and intimate relationship between inside and out were the defining components of this new tropical modernism.

The prestige of modern architecture also reached new levels with the creation of the capital city Brasília, one of the most fully realized visions of modern design and planning ever conceived. Brasília helped set Latin America's vibrant and innovative architectural culture in motion, and today the continent is still home to some of the world's most acclaimed contemporary architects. Most notably, the patterns of land use and planning—as well as economic conditions that have preserved a moneyed and culturally engaged middle class—have witnessed a steady stream of spectacular private houses created in the region. Often, the skewed socioeconomics and frequently turbulent politics of the region have resulted in unique archetypes, for better or for worse. The townhouse complexes of São Paolo, for example, with their self-contained domestic landscapes—insulated against the noise, traffic, and potential crime of the city outside—have allowed for striking, albeit exclusive, architectural expressions. Similarly, the ability to build amid dramatic, secluded landscapes, whether densely forested or spectacularly mountainous, is a privilege available only to a tiny percentage of the population.

3 The bold colors and generous spatial arrangements of Luis Barragán helped bring new perspectives to modern architecture, far removed from its European origins. This is the Cuadra San Cristóbal in Mexico City, built by Barragán in 1968.

Some of the most memorable recent architecture in Latin America has its roots in such privilege, a long haul from the fervent socialism of an architect such as Niemeyer (a long-time Communist Party member). Mexico City's new Museo Soumaya, designed by Fernando Romero and completed in 2011, was bankrolled by the billionaire Carlos Slim and houses a substantial proportion of his private art collection. In stark contrast, but no less architecturally adventurous, are the projects of Giancarlo Mazzanti in Medellín, Colombia, a city that has been transformed by architectural interventions. For example, Mazzanti's iconic Biblioteca España, three dark faceted cubes dramatically rising up above the flowing sprawl of the steep city streets, is a new symbol for Latin America and a far cry from the meticulous white forms of Niemeyer.

The Internet has given fresh prominence to countries that were once overshadowed by the cultural dominance of Brazil. Today, Chile, Argentina, Paraguay, and Bolivia are all home to thriving architecture cultures, with a new generation of young practitioners finding new opportunities. In 2016, the Chilean architect and educator Alejandro Aravena won the Pritzker Prize, the preeminent global award for architecture. Aravena and his studio, Elemental, gained recognition for their ultra-pragmatic approach to architecture. Their Quinta Monroy project was effectively "half-finished" housing, with space for additional elements to be added as and when they were needed. By applying standardization to an *ad hoc* form of construction that has underpinned low-income communities around the world for generations, Elemental could improve basic functions and livability, without compromising the fragile economic system of ultralow-cost housing. It seems that contemporary architecture in the region is finally reflecting Latin America's diversity of experience.

MEXICO CITY

Mexico City is going through something of a cultural and architectural renaissance, and the days of dangerous streets and rampant pollution are slowly being left behind. With money injected into the city through a growing economy and a fast-emerging, more affluent middle class, as well as a flourishing art and design scene and a thoroughly metropolitan attitude, the Mexican capital's cultural cachet is on the rise.

This is good news for the city, as it experienced phenomenal growth in the twentieth century that swiftly led to all sorts of problems. Not long ago, Mexico City was one of the most polluted urban centers in its region, if not the world. The city's housing grew hand in hand with its population, starting off by sprawling out and then building upward—the Torre Latinoamericana is not only one of the city's most recognizable landmarks, but also one of its oldest skyscrapers, completed in 1956. Shanty towns also began to form during the second half of the twentieth century, to house the working classes who provided the manpower needed to support

the city's tremendous growth. Consuming lakes, hills, and plains, Greater Mexico City engulfed everything in its path, transforming into what it is today: one of the top ten largest cities in the world.

Considering its rate and manner of growth, it comes as no surprise that Mexico City is composed of a real mix of historical and new—although not always top quality—architecture. During the big urban boom, many wealthier neighborhoods were pushed out into the suburbs, where architects experimented with designing lush modern villas and grand detached family houses. Areas such as San Angel—originally villages outside Mexico City, but then forced to join Greater Mexico City as it expanded—are a good example, filled with architectural treasures in a variety of styles, including the modernist home of Frida Kahlo and Diego Rivera. Jardines del Pedregal is another notable example, a neighborhood of ultramodern, upscale villas conceived by the well-known Mexican modernist Luis Barragán and created within lava fields. Originally developed in the 1940s, it was one of the era's major aspirational real-estate projects.

There are, however, some residential areas closer to the city center: the borough of Miguel Hidalgo, where the Barragán house and studio can be found, is part of Mexico City's oldest neighborhood. Located just next to the chic bars and restaurants of the central La Condesa district, it is now filled with townhouses for the middle classes. Still, the largest chunk of the city's urban development of the past decades took place in the suburbs.

Despite the recent economic downturn, the Mexican capital has cleaned up its act in an impressive way. Today, Greater Mexico City is a true global capital, home to more than 20 million people. It prides itself on having one of the strongest economies in Latin America and is the largest Spanish-speaking megacity in the world. This does not mean that its troubles are entirely in the past, as housing challenges—including a large quantity of low-quality housing—persist. However, projects such as architect Tatiana Bilbao's prototype "urgent" housing units—low-cost, light, adaptable, and efficient constructions designed to address Mexico's social accommodation shortage—begin to offer solutions to some of the city's, and wider country's, residential woes.

Mexico City's prominence in the art and design fields is also increasing. New and revamped festivals, such as Material Art Fair and Mexico Design Week, regularly highlight local established and emerging talent. A flourishing art scene not only means that more local artists stay and operate in the city, such as the award-winning Pedro Reyes, but also that the city's arsenal of cultural offerings is swiftly improving—and some of architecture's best have created landmark buildings to fit the booming industry. Fernando Romero's architecture and design firm FR-EE was behind one of the latest additions, the sleek and shimmering Museo Soumaya, completed in 2011. A little later, in 2013, British architect David Chipperfield completed the nearby Museo Jumex, which currently holds one of the largest art collections in Latin America.

The architecture scene is equally powerful. With established offices such as Ricardo Legorreta's studio still active, and a legacy of regional modernists such as Barragán, Félix Candela, and Pedro Ramírez Vázquez providing inspiration, many of Mexico's once-emerging practices have now grown into maturity—and most of them are based in the capital. Romero, Bilbao, Michel Rojkind, and Enrique Norten are all part of a generation currently changing the face of Mexico City. Smaller firms, such as DCPP, Jose Juan Rivera Rio, and Cadaval & Solà-Morales, are often busy in the residential field, working on both housing blocks and low-rise family homes that range in styles and budget, but all maintain a strong connection with the outdoors, opening up to courtyards, gardens, and terraces.

Important new public projects are still in the works, by both local and foreign names. Foster + Partners has teamed up with Fernando Romero for a new city airport and Richard Meier is

1 In "new" Latin America, Museo Soumaya (2011), designed by FR-EE, is a private museum paid for by the billionaire Carlos Slim to house his many art collections. 2 Luis Barragán's own house in Mexico City was completed in 1948. He lived there until his death in 1988, and it is now on the UNESCO World Heritage list.

3   4

3   Torre Latinoamericana was designed by Augusto H. Álvarez.   4   The Diego Rivera and Frida Kahlo House Studio Museum in Mexico City was designed by Juan O'Gorman.

planning mixed-use complexes, such as the sleek Reforma Towers. New cultural spaces are appearing, too, including the Archivo art and architecture gallery by Zeller & Moye (overseen by Romero) and the Alumnos 47 art foundation's new home by Didier Faustino. The ripple effect of all this activity is felt across all architectural sectors.

The city's housing, though, is a true reflection of its history and growing fortunes. Preserved colonial-style mansions sit hand in hand with modernist experiments, while on the more contemporary front, an emerging generation of architects work on defining what modern Mexican architecture means. Adapting traditional styles to contemporary needs, and international movements to regional customs and the local climate, Mexico City's dynamic practices are forging their way to a better, more considered urban realm.

CASA ALPES

Casa Alpes is a radical reconstruction and extension of an original 1950s modernist villa, undoing decades of insensitive alterations that had damaged the original character of the building. Located in the exclusive Lomas de Chapultepec colonia (neighborhood) of Mexico City, the house is generously scaled, totaling around 10,225 square feet (950 sq m). The street elevation is relatively modest, however, with a blank ceramic-clad wall rising up above new metal security gates. There is little hint of the scope or scale of the space contained within. This enclosed approach to domestic urban design is a common characteristic of South American architecture, where residences regularly present an understated public facade, saving the spatial dynamics for the interior realm.

Casa Alpes is raised up above its entrance level, which is dedicated to parking, garage space, plant, and service areas. As a result, the primary living spaces begin at level one, thus increasing the amount of available light and privacy. A slender but generously long 80-foot (25 m) swimming pool delineates the edge of the site, while the airy open-plan living room, dining area, and kitchen are arranged around the walled courtyard garden that surrounds the property. From within, the views are green and lively, albeit also self contained. During the refurbishment, the architects added new metal columns in order to open up the living spaces even further, and also to help the house comply with the increasingly stringent local earthquake regulations.

Both the pool and a new roof terrace were additions to the program, as were the service areas in the front courtyard. On the top floor, the city views open out and the quiet anonymity of the street facade is forgotten. "The project rescues the modern spirit of the original house but avoids any historical mimicry," the architects say. Material choices were especially important. The front facade uses handmade ceramic tiles locally sourced in Guadalajara, while internal finishes utilize a sparing mix of iconic modern materials—stainless steel, concrete, oak, and Bakelite—to exploit different textures and details without compromising the sense of space.

1 A new roof terrace offers an expansive urban vista.   2 The pool sits alongside a fully glazed living space.   3 There is also a secondary living area at the other end of the house.   4 From the street, Casa Alpes presents a mysterious, white ceramic facade.

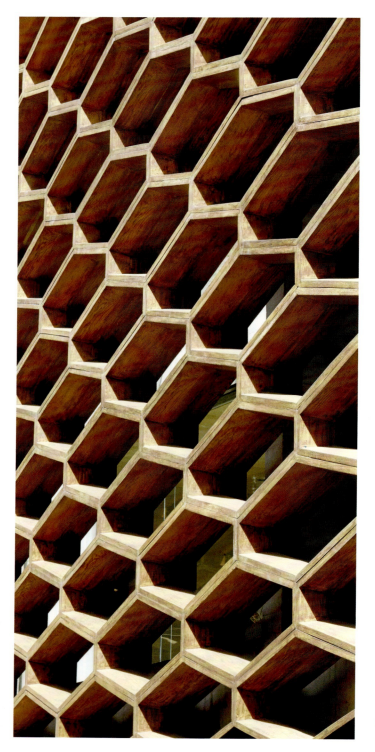

CASA ROEL

In urban settings, it is not uncommon to be faced with an awkward plot, where architects have to work with small or strangely shaped sites, squeezed by neighboring buildings from all sides. However, these challenging situations often offer the most fertile ground for inspired design solutions. This was the case for Felipe Assadi and Francisca Pulido's Casa Roel in Mexico City, which they completed in collaboration with Mexican architect Isaac Broid.

Wanting to create an efficient internal arrangement, but also make the most of the region's pleasant weather, the architects worked with an H-shaped floor plan, alternating closed and open-air spaces. This led to a volumetric composition that hints at Mexico City's historical courtyard housing. Working with the H-shaped footprint, the architects created two concrete pavilions placed parallel to one another, linked by a third one, which acts as a bridge and allows the two main wings of the house to communicate. This generated several open-air terraces and gardens in between the built volumes, establishing a strong dialogue between inside and out. The pavilion that sits closest to the street contains the house's common areas—the living room, dining room, and kitchen—tucked behind a honeycomb-shaped perforated screen. The bedrooms are located within the two pavilions toward the rear of the site, which are set back from the street to ensure privacy. Underneath the main house are the garage, a workshop, and a series of service spaces.

As the site is located on a slope, the architects decided to lift the whole concrete structure on stilts in order to negotiate the steep level change. This led to the creation of a wealth of different clearings and patios around and under the house, which have been planted with rich vegetation, forming part of Casa Roel's lush gardens. Greenery peeks out from the most unexpected of places, such as by a staircase or the bathroom, and in between different parts of the house. Making use of the structure's roof, by planting it and adding a deck and a swimming pool, is the house's hidden bonus. This extra space provides the perfect vantage point from which the residents can sit back and take in the panoramic views of Mexico City.

1 A honeycomb-shaped perforated screen filters in light.
2 Casa Roel has an H-shaped footprint.   3 A slim concrete staircase leads up to a roof terrace.   Overleaf Living spaces are protected by the external screen and greenery.

SÃO PAULO

Brazil's rich legacy in architecture is the stuff of modernist dreams. During the twentieth century, the country was the playground of some of the most prominent architects in the world, with international icons such as Oscar Niemeyer, Lina Bo Bardi, Ruy Ohtake, and Paulo Mendes da Rocha becoming synonymous with what was widely recognized as Brazilian—or tropical—modern architecture. With Niemeyer only recently departing this world (the centenarian architect passed away in 2012 at the age of 104) and other influential figures such as Mendes da Rocha still going strong, the burden and privilege of responding to this heritage fell squarely on the shoulders of the younger generation of architects operating in the country today.

They have plenty to work with: a country rich in natural resources and materials, a wealth of traditional building techniques to choose from—both indigenous and imported, fittingly reflecting Brazil's multicultural population—and a varied climate and geography. They also need to define themselves against what their predecessors—in many cases, their teachers—created. Faced with such challenges, this contemporary wave of Brazilian architects responded with flair and ambition. Marcio Kogan, Isay Weinfeld, Marcelo Ferraz, and Angelo Bucci are but a few of this prolific generation that has already left its stamp on the country's residential scene.

Brazil's current crop of architecture practices experiment and produce houses of all shapes and sizes, throughout the width and breadth of the country, embracing but also developing further the key characteristics that make the Brazilian genre so recognizable. Their residential work often features open plans and large openings, flat roofs, a seamless weaving of indoors and outdoors, tactile materials such as concrete and wood, and rich, tropical gardens. Merging different architectural traditions, the country has produced some of the most striking houses in the world.

Unfortunately, this legacy has been growing hand in hand with the country's wide sociopolitical and economic problems. On the opposite end of the spectrum that saw wealthy patrons commission architects on the cutting edge to design dramatic villas and private museums sit Brazil's millions of underprivileged citizens, who are forced to make do with makeshift homes and off-the-grid tenements. Nowhere in the country has this been more prominent than in São Paulo. This global metropolis, while technically not the country's capital—the white curves of Brasília reserve the privilege to that title—is without doubt Brazil's undisputed architectural heart. Cultural and fiscal capital merge in this most vibrant of cities to offer one of the most varied and rich architectural landscapes in Brazil, the fifth-largest country in the world.

The city's wealth of modernist offerings includes cultural and commercial work—the São Paulo Museum of Modern Art in Ibirapuera Park by Niemeyer, and Lina Bo Bardi's Sesc Pompéia are notable examples—as well as a selection of large-scale multifamily housing blocks. Many are lovingly preserved and restored by architecturally aware apartment owners. Examples range from the iconic Edifício Copan by Niemeyer (home to more than 1,000 apartments) to the nineteen-story Edifício Bretagne in Higienópolis, by Artacho Jurado. There is plenty of smaller-scale housing, too. From generous townhouses to opulent villas, single-family houses can be found all over São Paulo—and are not confined to upmarket neighborhoods such as Jardins, home to some of the city's best museums, stores, and restaurants. The more bohemian area of Vila Madalena is a great example of where the aspiring middle class of São Paulo likes to set up shop. Many emerging dynamic architects have premises there, such as the trio behind FGMF—Fernando Forte, Lourenço Gimenes, and Rodrigo Marcondes Ferraz—thereby making this neighborhood one of the city's most vibrant and creative hubs.

However, this sprawling megacity is also home to great swathes of subquality housing, including more than fifty of Brazil's infamous

1 Oscar Niemeyer's Edifício Copan was built in 1966. With thirty-eight stories and 1,160 apartments, it is one of the largest buildings in Brazil.   2 São Paulo is a city of contrasts, with its modern architecture sitting side by side with its infamous favelas.

avelas. The city's rapid growth during the past century, combined with financial, political, and social problems, gave birth to all kinds of urbanistic issues, such as low-quality housing clusters, high pollution rates, and dreadful circulation—the super rich of São Paulo famously prefer to travel to their appointments by helicopter, in order to avoid the incredible congestion at street level. As in many places in Brazil, supreme wealth goes hand in hand with shanty towns in São Paulo.

The city's lingering inequalities and slums have been highlighted by many local politicians as a priority challenge, and building new modern housing for its most underprivileged citizens is part of the solution, as is safeguarding the often valuable land they sit on. Many of the city's architects have been working toward designing better public accommodation for Brazil's largest city. Jardim Edite Social Housing Complex, designed by MMBB and H+F Arquitetos and completed in 2010, offers a glimpse of what São Paulo's social housing of the future could look like.

3 São Paulo's clusters... quality housing are only one of its urbanistic problems; traffic congestion and pollution are also key issues that architects and local authorities are keen to tackle. 4 The Jardim Edite Social Housing Complex comprises 525 homes. Promoted by the Ministry of Housing, the complex has a nursery, health service unit, and school.

SÃO PAULO

COUNTRY Brazil
ARCHITECT AR Arquitetos   **YEAR** 2012

1 Windows of various sizes are cut out of Patio House's white facade, bringing in ample light.   2 One of the architects' key design gestures was to create a dramatic living room.

PATIO HOUSE

Patio House is more than a creative re-imagining of a 1950s house in a dense urban neighborhood; it is an exercise in crafting a residence with a seamless circulation system that effortlessly merges indoors and outdoors, faithful to Brazil's tropical modern tradition.

São Paulo-based practice AR Arquitetos—headed by Marina Acayaba and Juan Pablo Rosenberg—was called upon to work on the complete remodeling of an existing building in the heart of the city's Vila Madalena district. Faced with a structure of no particular architectural value, a rather crammed internal program of small cellular rooms, and a poor circulation system, the team had to think outside the box. Taking inspiration from Gordon Matta-Clark's "building cuts" and James Turrell's Skyspaces, AR Arquitetos redesigned the house as a simple white volume, albeit with a twist. By inserting two courtyards within the main body and cutting out several rectangular windows that now dot the facade, the architects

opened up and completely transformed the original house's unrefined interior. These clearings act as "decompression areas," while the different windows look out toward the garden, the patios and, internally, to various rooms in the house, thereby improving visual connections. Instead of demolishing the structure and rebuilding it, which would have been time consuming and costly, they decided to treat the existing building as an urban ruin, a "solid to be excavated."

The first courtyard is a double-height space on the first floor, featuring a tree that grows green between the family room and the children's room. The second one serves as the master bedroom's private terrace. Both spaces were placed with care and precision within the whole, positioned to frame specific views through levels and across rooms that encourage privacy where needed, but also interaction between family members. A further void is cut internally

through the structure and reaches down to the lower ground level—where the old garage used to be—allowing natural light to flood inside the building and transforming the space into a bright and airy double-height living room.

A traditional approach to the internal arrangement means that public spaces—for living, kitchen, and dining—are located on the ground level, leading out to a garden that wraps around the house, allowing room to breathe within its dense urban setting. Private spaces—the family room, play area, bathrooms, and three bedrooms—occupy the first and second floors of this smartly arranged modern renovation. Timber floors and decking throughout contrast the building's white walls and add domestic warmth to the geometric composition.

3 Two patios in different parts of the house act as light shafts to brighten up the interiors.   4 The views through rooms and across levels create unexpected visual connections.

CASA DOS PÁTIOS

Set in a forested suburb and designed by acclaimed architect Isay Weinfeld, who has achieved global recognition for his sensitive but dramatic updating of traditional Brazilian modernist tropes, Casa dos Pátios is the quintessential architectural re-imagining of the São Paulo suburban house. Here, a traditional family unit of four is given seemingly infinite space in a conventional and slightly restricted long, narrow plot. An underground garage and workshop free up the ground floor for living space. The main house is generously scaled, although not imposing, with a first floor shaped like a traditional pitched roof structure—almost the archetypal house form—extruded along the length of the site. This sits above a classic Weinfeld device: a ground floor comprised of courtyards, glass walls, and full-height sliding glass doors, with living spaces spilling out into the garden and vice versa. As a result, there are verdant views from every living space.

The house is entered via a long green corridor beneath a wooden pergola, taking the owners and visitors right into the heart of the plan and revealing the garden courtyard. At the far end of the site is a wedge-shaped, free-standing structure with a gym and sauna on the ground floor and a self-contained guest suite above. The first floor overhangs the courtyard garden, providing shade for the barbecue and seating area. There is also a slender pool in the main courtyard, while limestone floors unite the interior and exterior spaces. Up above, the four bedrooms are far more private, with window shutters that match the wooden facade. A private family room and two terraces complete the generous accommodation.

Like many grand private houses in São Paulo, Casa dos Pátios is inward looking and self contained, partly for security reasons. A solid concrete basement and ground floor are mixed with a steel-framed first floor to enable the cantilever above the garden. The pitched roof has a mix of skylights and solar panels to maximize the house's autonomy and feeling of space.

1 A narrow walkway leads to the house.   2 The cantilevered first floor creates a shaded courtyard.   3 The living room and garden emphasize the generous horizontal spaces. Overleaf The dining room adjoins an internal courtyard.

CASA COBOGÓ

While there are common threads running through most narratives that involve building in an urban environment—often linked to issues of density, privacy, and connecting with the outdoors—geography plays an equally important role in residential design. Being able to adapt to the climate and different cultural needs is essential in creating architectural success stories, and often means embracing traditional regional skills and techniques, and reinventing them for the twenty-first century. This is the approach that Brazilian architect Marcio Kogan and his team at Studio mk27 chose for Casa Cobogó.

Built for Brazil's temperate climate, in the bustling metropolis of São Paulo, this house encompasses several key characteristics of the tropical modern home. Its ground floor, comprising two generous living spaces, a kitchen and a dining area, opens up toward the surrounding garden. Large glass walls draw back to lead out to terraces, a small artificial lake, and greenery, thus seamlessly merging indoors and outdoors. The first floor contains the private rooms—bedrooms and bathrooms—lined in warm woods that offset the house's hard concrete shell and create a softer atmosphere against the ground level's tiled floor. Bedrooms are protected from the sun and prying eyes by operable lattice wooden panels that filter light and views in. Not only working with but also protecting the surrounding environment, the architects used sustainable and energy-efficient systems where possible. There is, for example, a water recycling plant in place, in order to reduce water consumption, as well as solar panels to help satisfy heating needs.

However, the house's centerpiece is its elaborate top floor: a spacious gym and meditation room enveloped in white cobogó. Cobogós are a Brazilian feature, a merging of local Mediterranean and Arab architectural responses to the country's hot climate. The technique, which originated in Recife, involves building a perforated screen using cobogó blocks, to form a structure that

1 Marcio Kogan's signature modernist-inspired forms are evident in this house.   2 Perforated timber screens bring soft light upstairs, where the private areas are located.   3 The top level is dedicated to a studio room wrapped in cobogó walls.

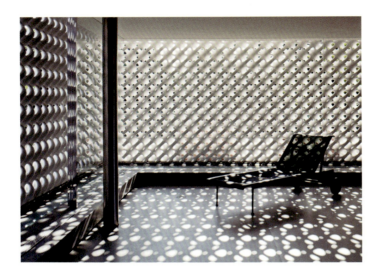

allows natural light and ventilation to come into the house, while ensuring privacy for the residents. At the same time, the lace-like pattern creates a soft play of shadows inside as the sun's rays penetrate the walls, building a distinct internal atmosphere. The method was widely used by Brazilian modernist Lúcio Costa, and was one of his signature gestures.

For Casa Cobogó, Studio mk27 used curvaceous concrete blocks designed by the Austrian-American Erwin Hauer and inspired by the smooth lines of Oscar Niemeyer. The resulting white crown is the perfect topping for this family home: bright and breezy during the day and delicately shining like a lantern at night, when lit from within.

4 Studio mk27 drew on traditional local techniques for natural air and light circulation.   5 The screens can be drawn back completely.   6 When the weather allows, the ground level becomes one with the garden.

CASA CIEN

Chilean architects Mauricio Pezo and Sofia von Ellrichshausen have built an international reputation for creating striking minimalist villas. Their portfolio is awash with monolithic residences that form bold architectural statements against the breathtaking natural landscapes of Chile. One of their very first offerings, Casa Poli—a summer house and cultural center perched on a hillside overlooking the ocean—was their breakthrough project, placing them firmly on the world architecture map in 2005. They have been going from strength to strength with new house projects ever since.

Their designs use powerful and clean geometric shapes that, at first glance, may appear as if they would look at their best only within the natural wilderness, but this is not necessarily the case—and Casa Cien, one of the pair's most recent completions, proves this point. Nestled within a generous sloped site of 10,010 square feet (930 sq m), this project is situated in a suburb of the city of Concepción, where the practice is based. In fact, the seven-story tower houses the architecture couple's own residence and studio space. The building is formed of a single slender tower sat on a long, low podium. While this plinth allows the interior to extend visually into the garden, through its large openings that ensure direct contact with the outside, the tower feels somewhat detached from the ground, with its rooms firmly focused toward the vistas that turn the gaze to the city, hills and ocean in the distance.

The composition's distinct shape was not a random decision nor an architectural folly. The architects count "the number of steps on a hill path nearby, the statue of an old cypress reminiscent of those described by the art critic Walter Pater, or even the whole number of the elevation above sea level that defines the podium" as elements that may playfully explain the building's silhouette. However, the final design was based on a game of spatial experimentation; the architects used a square unit of fixed size as their module and tried to repeat and rearrange it across all floors. Each of these

units holds four main areas, which are positioned in a different configuration on every level, adjusted to cater to each space's needs, ranging from a study to living rooms and rest areas.

The work spaces are placed on the lower floor, while the residential element is spread across the middle and top levels. Different staircases offer access to these two functions. The exterior's rough exposed concrete is matched inside by timber floors, cabinetry and detailing, some of it left natural and some painted. This softens somewhat the house's overall Brutalist feel. Different-sized windows in galvanized steel dot the facade, framing the garden and city views beyond.

5 Warm timber floors on some levels offset the concrete's roughness.   6 Casa Cien is Mauricio Pezo and Sofia von Ellrichshausen's Concepción base.   7 The plinth, which houses the studio, is strongly connected to the outdoors.

BUENOS AIRES

COUNTRY Argentina
ARCHITECT Nicolás Pinto da Mota / Victoria María Falcón   YEAR 2017

CASA ESQUINA

Located in one of Buenos Aires' low-rise residential suburbs, Casa Esquina occupies a prominent corner site. Traditionally, the single-family housing in this area is set back from the edges of the lots, with parking areas and small front gardens. The 30- by 43-foot (9 x 13 m) plot is also adjacent to a neighboring park, offering up the potential for green views despite the urban location.

The architects describe the house as being first and foremost about shape and volume, and how these relate to the continuity of the existing urban family. Corner sites are a key part of successful urban design, and Casa Esquina's prominent location next to a crossroads offered up a number of possible approaches. Arranged as a series of terraces and setbacks on the upper floor, in order to maximize views of the park, the house "turns" the corner with its handsome light brick elevations, subtly modulated with inset windows, doors, and patterning to define the boundaries of the plot

and hint at the interior arrangements. The secondary bedrooms are all located on the ground floor, along with the bathrooms and a playroom, while the main suite of living rooms is on the L-shaped first floor, with a square terrace given a prominent spot on the corner. A linear kitchen is set alongside a formal drawing room, with the staircase set in the edge of the plan furthest from the street. The top floor is given over to the parents' bedroom, bathroom, and study area, with two covered terraces overlooking the park.

The brick and concrete finishes play to the strengths of regional skills and building techniques. They also have a monolithic quality that "better expresses the idea of permanence," according to architects Nicolás Pinto da Mota and Victoria María Falcón. Casa Esquina is a house that acknowledges the wider city, through the intersection of its open volumes with the streetscape and in its heavy brick design, which forms an anchor for the neighborhood.

CASA MG

Natural light and a sense of openness were two of architect Joan Marantz's key concerns when redesigning this single-family house in Buenos Aires. The commission for Casa MG—also known as Terrace House—outlined the complete re-imagining of an existing townhouse, and in particular the transformation of its roof terrace into an outdoor haven. Marantz wanted to create a single, open, and flowing space—especially on the ground level, which hosts the entrance hall and the key living areas. This part of the building used to be divided into several fairly small, dark rooms. By knocking down existing walls, three main spaces were created to cater for the kitchen, dining, and sitting rooms. This simple gesture enhanced visual connections across different areas and levels, while allowing light to seep deep into the structure.

The material selection was important to create the architect's desired overall feel of warmth and functionality, and to keep costs within the available budget. The exterior is clad in light-colored wood, matched by pine and polished concrete inside. A central circulation patio guides visitors from the street to the main living areas, and a second staircase at the back—within an impressive double-height space—leads to the upper floor's terrace: the house's true centerpiece. This is the element that defines the new design and also inspired the house's name.

The open-air rooftop (previously a neglected part of the building) now features a sculptural white canopy—playfully taking the shape of an abstract, archetypal house—decked resting areas, a grill, and a garden. Planted areas are matched by lively entertainment spaces that during the warm months become an extension of the downstairs family room. The streamlined design bears the signature of its architect's overall approach, which favors function and sustainability. At the same time, the structure's light elegant forms and efficient design create the perfect urban oasis for this cleverly conceived inner-city townhouse renovation project.

1 This house's standout feature is its roof terrace, which includes decked and planted areas.   2 The sculptural white canopy playfully hints at a pitched roof.   Overleaf During the warm months, the roof terrace becomes an extension of the living room.

CASA EN EL AIRE

Casa en el Aire (House in the Air) is, as its name suggests, raised up above a small site in the Paraguayan city of Luque, an eastern suburb of Asunción. Its plot is long and thin, created out of the end of three existing gardens. The new house follows the basic topography of the site, using fine structural and mechanical details to weave a building out of solid concrete and ceramic-faced walls.

The structure is pared back into two key elements: one block containing the stair and the other the bathrooms and services. These components also contain the concealed structure that holds up the cantilevered living spaces, and acts as a literal shield to protect the new house from being overlooked by surrounding properties and the worst of the region's weather. Clad with ceramic roofing tiles, these blocks have a monumental form, especially when contrasted with the verdant garden surroundings. The clients' restricted budget required lateral thinking, as did the climatic demands of a site where high summer temperatures are paired with northeasterly prevailing winds and cold winters that see polar winds come up from the south. "These elements give us the keys to rethink a better space," the architects say, "the lack of economic resources is often the tool that drives us to reformulate solutions to problems that with a bigger budget we could not even imagine."

By diverting the structure and services into the two "barrier" blocks, a large percentage of the site area was freed up. The architects created a huge horizontal concrete slab, 52 by 16 feet (16 x 5 m), beneath the cantilevered living area, thereby forming an indoor/outdoor space that can serve as a terrace, car port, barbecue area, or simple covered open space, depending on the season. The elaborate tropical planting to the north of the site gives this garden patio an enclosed, sheltered quality, which makes it feel like an extension of the living spaces above. The entire structure is arranged around four pairs of slim pillars, and the living space itself is raised 9 feet (2.8 m)

1 A long strip of windows brings light into the kitchen, sitting room, and master bedroom.   2 The main building blocks of the house are clearly visible, a ceramic-clad service structure at left, off which the concrete living areas are hung.

above the garden. The east and west elevations have no windows, but the 52-foot (16 m) strip of glass in the living space—running the entire width of the facade—brings natural light into the kitchen, sitting room, and master bedroom. This window has a complex mechanism of opening panes. It also illuminates the long counter that serves as a work desk and kitchen worktop. Finally, the house's flat roof is also a generous terrace with views across the surrounding area. From certain angles, Casa en el Aire appears mysterious and almost foreboding. Ultimately, it is a structural response to site, materials, and climate.

3 · 4

3 The house's location at the end of existing gardens means that it needs to be protected from being overlooked as well as from the wind. 4 Below the house is a sheltered courtyard and seating area, surrounded by tropical planting.

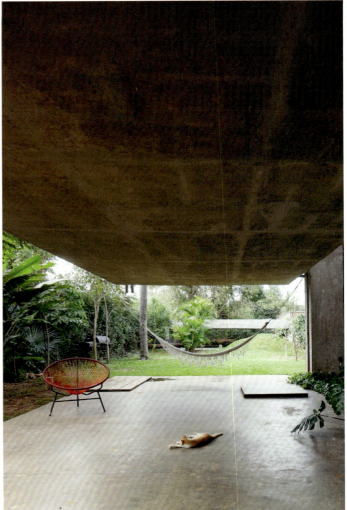

1

1 Amsterdam's Inntel Hotel by WAM Architecten plays on the vernacular forms of traditional Dutch housing, stacking colorful gabled facades on top of each other.

EUROPE

STAVANGER HELSINKI DUBLIN
LONDON PARIS ROTTERDAM
BRUSSELS FRANKFURT STÄFA
PORTO BARCELONA VARESE
ATHENS MOSCOW

2 A pioneering piece of urban postmodernism, albeit on a smaller scale, FAT's Blue House in East London incorporates a scaled-down cityscape in its decorative facade.

Europe is the birthplace of modernism, home to the Bauhaus and the center from which the contemporary vision of architecture—in materials, form, and program—spread around the world. It is also an agglomeration of fifty countries with millennia of history between them, as well as every conceivable type of habitat, terrain, and culture. Modern architecture is often described as a homogenizer, a universal approach to a problem that has evolved in myriad different ways.

For a brief moment, it was true that there was a sense of unity, purpose, and shared vision among the modernists (perhaps best highlighted in publications such as F. R. S. Yorke's *The Modern House*, which appeared in many editions throughout the 1930s and 1940s). However, that was soon fractured by war and a creative diaspora unlike any other. The traditional narrative has the modernists and their ideas spread to the four winds, then closely involved with the postwar rebuilding project, most notably in Europe. In among the deprivation and necessity, the individual private house could only ever be a creative footnote, but it still retained its status as the preeminent way of conveying architectural ideologies.

After the first spectacular flourish of the International Style, there was a slow but burgeoning revival of respect and interest in the vernacular, which gradually crept back into the architectural vocabulary of Europe's culturally disparate nations. In Scandinavian countries, the strict white-walled modernism was never taken up with as much enthusiasm as it was elsewhere. There, from the 1930s onward, a warmer and less austere style of architecture took root, inverting the new architecture's recommendation of more interaction between inside and out by placing a greater emphasis on interior layout and the non-hierarchical arrangement of the home. Ultimately, dogma was defeated by design. Modernism's apotheosis was to be found in minimalism, a purist, pared-back version of the architectural approach espoused by Walter Gropius, Le Corbusier, Ludwig Mies van der Rohe, and others, which had little to do with light, space, health, wellness, and social betterment but almost everything to do with a post-materialist anti-display of status. It was modern and beautiful, but it said little about architecture's ability to make a difference.

The postwar housing crisis was tackled, with varying degrees of success, by the arrival of the postwar apartment building. Many architects and engineers believed that the house itself could benefit from the intensive and expanded production capacity left over from the war effort, and that houses could be built along the same lines as bombers and tanks. Prefabrication seemed like a natural process for postwar reconstruction, and several architects, most notably the Frenchman Jean Prouvé and the American Richard Buckminster Fuller, threw themselves into engineering houses as if they were furniture, finished with sleek metal panels and designed to be light, demountable, and transportable to all corners of the globe.

In the United Kingdom, prefabrication had little of the design kudos or technological zest of its continental rivals, but it was successful, to a degree. Just over 150,000 examples of modest bungalow prefabs were constructed on former bomb sites, many of which survived decades longer than intended. In contrast, Prouvé took the Corbusian maxim that a "house is a machine for living in" to an engineered conclusion, creating beautifully detailed structures that were far too expensive. In the modern era, the Parisian gallerist Patrick Seguin transformed the utilitarian into art, selling single-room Prouvé-designed structures for many millions of dollars to collectors and aesthetes who treat them as livable sculptures. Finland was also interested in the potential of prefabrication, and projects such as the summer house created by Marimekko and Matti Suuronen's Futuro House, a UFO-like plastic structure designed in the late 1960s, tapped into the aesthetic zeitgeist but ultimately failed as commercial projects.

Modernism also faced aesthetic opposition. A revival of interest in Neoclassicism and decorative design, especially in the United Kingdom, Italy and France, ultimately manifested itself as postmodernism, a movement that celebrated the human scale of classical forms and details. Postmodernism could be playful and warm, most especially when used as a form of juxtaposition, as seen in FAT's Blue House in East London, Charles Jencks and Terry Farrell's early Victorian villa in Holland Park, or even WAM Architecten's Inntel Hotel in Amsterdam, the last of which appears as a stacked cube of traditional Dutch housing.

3 The Bilbao Guggenheim by Frank Gehry, which opened in 1997, is often hailed as a milestone in modern town planning for its use of culture as a magnet to generate investment and social capital.

Yet ultimately, the best received iteration of contemporary design has been that which appeared during the mid-century period, when vernacular forms and traditional materials were incorporated into contemporary designs for living. The mature, refined modernism of the Scandinavian countries was perhaps the most successful at adapting itself to the local climate and culture, all without losing respect for tradition and integration into the landscape or city.

Europe is also the birthplace of the architectural icon, the cultural trophy that usurped the skyscraper as the preeminent demonstration of architecture as power. Most historians—cultural and architectural—point to the opening of the Bilbao Guggenheim, designed by Canadian-American architect Frank Gehry, in 1997 in Spain as the moment of change. It is no exaggeration to say that, from this occasion onward, the city once again saw architecture as a focal point, not necessarily as part of grand axial planning but as a magnet to attract visitors, investment, and economic growth.

What effect did this have on residential design within the continent and beyond? It certainly prefigured a new boom in apartment building, particularly at the higher end of the market, which in many cases replaced usurped social housing. The long-term impact of such moves is still unclear, but the fact that many of the examples in this chapter show how economics shapes architectural innovation implies that the modern city is woefully out of kilter with the supply and demand of housing.

The contemporary European city is not especially conducive to the building of individual houses, having long since banished housing to the suburbs. However, the lure of location and the ability of architecture to eke out places to live from unpromising spaces continue to surprise and delight, proving that modern design can still make the most of space and light.

NORTH FACE HOUSE

Designing for urban environments—even sparsely built residential neighborhoods, such as this one in Norway's Stavanger—always means having to negotiate the existing built fabric, and sometimes involves directly engaging with part of it. Restorations, renovations, and extensions are many an architect's bread and butter, but that does not mean that bold, creative solutions are out of the question.

North Face House, by Element Arkitekter, is an imaginative redesign of an existing 1969 structure built as part of a twin set of residences sitting next to each other. Although the plot offered a generous footprint and long views—thanks to a steeply sloped site and a north-facing aspect toward the sea, which lends the house its name—the project's clients were after a refresh. The aim was to rearrange and completely redesign the interior, so that it would better fit the demands of twenty-first-century living. The architects, an Oslo-based practice led by Cathrine Vigander and Vidar Knutsen, obliged. Keeping the structure's two lower stories, they decided to replace the top floor with something lighter and more modern. They also opened up a large window on the top floor, thus framing the water vistas and underlining the new design's openness.

In terms of the internal arrangement, the lower levels host the more private parts of the house, such as bedrooms and bathrooms, as well as service areas. The top floor is reserved for the open-plan living spaces, which reveal striking views toward Byfjorden fjord. This part of the house cantilevers over the rest by 10 feet (3 m). On the opposite side of the plot, the house is set back from the street, creating a large deck toward the south—an ideal orientation to capture the sun, while protected from the cold northern wind. An external skin of Kebony timber wraps around the new floor and extends down, uniting the old and new parts of the house. In an environmentally conscious approach, elements of the old building were reused in the construction, while the new parts were built in solid wood.

1 North Face House features a Kebony timber-clad top level.
2 The main living spaces look out toward Byfjorden fjord.
3 The extensive use of timber is seen in floors and staircases.
Overleaf The living room focuses on views across the water.

HELSINKI
COUNTRY Finland
ARCHITECT Tuomas Siitonen Office **YEAR** 2013

1 Set in an existing back garden, House M-M is a multigenerational home. 2 The double-height kitchen and living space form the heart of the house, where all generations can come together.

HOUSE M-M

House M-M is described by its architects as a contemporary interpretation of the traditional multigenerational dwelling. The brief harks back to earlier forms of social and family interaction, but the result adds a modernist twist in terms of planning and spatial arrangements. Designed by the Helsinki firm of Tuomas Siitonen, the new three-story building is set on a slope in one of the city's wooded suburbs and consists of two interlinked apartments in around 1,830 square feet (170 sq m) of space. "What if the whole extended family lived together, on the same plot, even under the same roof?" the architect asked rhetorically, when tasked with creating a home for two actors and their extended family, which included grandparents and a great-grandmother. The brief not only called for shared family space but also private areas, where everyone could do their own thing. In this way, each generation could help out and feel secure without constantly imposing on one another.

The site's topography helped Siitonen deliver all of the criteria. Located in Helsinki's Oulunkylä district, the plot formed part of a steeply sloping garden belonging to a century-old house. House M-M makes use of the contours to embed itself in the landscape, thus providing green views out of the large windows. The extensive use of wood in both the cladding and the structure creates the feeling of a tree house, with a high-ceilinged main living space and a lofty master bedroom located at the top. The exterior cladding is in Siberian larch, which gradually turns gray as it ages, while the interior wood, particularly in the bespoke kitchen, gives off a welcome warmth.

On the plot, the existing villa—also owned by the family—retains its local views thanks to a carefully placed dip in the roof of the new building. The floor plan of the new structure was angled so as to preserve the private characteristics of both parts of the garden, and also to shield it from the nearby public road. As a multigenerational

dwelling, the new house needed to have convenience as well as character. From a practical point of view, it contains an accessible ground-floor apartment, suitable for a person in their nineties, together with a communal family sauna and utility areas that serve the whole property. Above the ground floor, the space has been configured as an apartment for the clients and their two children. The main kitchen/reception area is lined in flamed birch, with space enough to cater for living and dining for the entire extended family. It also opens out onto a large terrace for the summer months.

Siitonen's design is extremely energy efficient, with a ground-source heat pump that does away with the need for conventional radiators. The large windows help with passive heating and ventilation, while a traditional open fireplace brings warmth and conviviality. The architect emphasizes the social value of this multigenerational model, in the face of a fast-aging population and the lack of childcare provision. "Well-designed models for multigenerational living and functional architecture can help meet these challenges in the future."

3 The site slopes steeply, so accommodation for the older generations is set at ground-floor level.   4 Wooden cladding is designed to weather and to become part of the landscape.

HOUSES 1&2

Multigenerational living is not uncommon in dense urban centers where space is at a premium, as this example of a double house for an extended family in Dublin demonstrates. Designed by TAKA Architects—established by Alice Casey and Cian Deegan in Bangladesh in 2006—Houses 1 & 2 are located in a quiet residential street of the Irish capital, among an existing row of Victorian houses. The project, explain the architects, involved "two new homes to house two generations of the same family: a renovated Victorian house for the parents, sharing a rear garden with a new mews house for one of their daughters."

While the design allows for extra space for the now grown-up family to expand further and have room to breathe, it also ensures that a strong link remains between the family members, and that a sense of spatial and historical continuity is maintained at the same time within both the site and the residents' daily lives. In order to achieve this, the architects sought to use familiar objects and domestic references within the new design.

The fireplace becomes the central focus of the new mews home, with an industrial-sized chimney soaring through the building and thus defining the spaces within. Reflecting the daughter's memories of the stairway as another "room" in her old house, the new enlarged staircase has spaces for contemplation, while the kitchen maintains the social character it had when the family was smaller and younger, in its role as the heart of the home. All these elements are woven into the new mews house in an exaggerated form that highlights and celebrates their importance.

Although the new spaces feel modern and updated, both houses' functions are traditional and remain true to the family's collective memories, thereby allowing for familiar events such as the family's Sunday gatherings to continue in the parents' new home. Several built-in elements underline the relevance of these key spaces. "Cast in concrete, the altar-like dining table communicates its importance through immovable materiality," say the architects, for example. Houses 1 & 2, which span a total of 4,305 square feet (400 sq m),

1 The kitchen constitutes a key social part of the project.
2 The two houses share a garden, which visually connects the living spaces. 3 Houses 1 & 2 is a multigenerational project, involving a renovated house and a new mews house.

4 The whole complex features distinctive elaborate brick facades.   5 The intricate brickwork was laid in a pattern dictated by the bricklayer.

have their main living areas on the ground level. A shared garden acts as a bridge between them—a mix of leafy and paved parts— while the complex's characteristic brick facade unifies the design. This intricate brickwork, laid in a random pattern chosen by the bricklayer, serves as a beautifully crafted ornamentation but at the same time forms part of the building's very construction.

In this case study, architecture not only provides physical space and delivers the means for a family to grow and occupy a building in a different way, but also plays a pivotal role in reinforcing and defining what a family unit can mean.

LONDON

In terms of the quality, space, and location of housing, modern London is a city of searing contrasts between rich and poor. Shaped by centuries of house building, the capital is often described as an agglomeration of villages, each characterized by a particular period or style. As a result, London is a city that was built on speculation and the vagaries of the market. From the Georgian era onward, new housing was built not to order but to demand, with master builders making their fortune by transforming gardens and farms into the terraces and squares of the new metropolis. With the coming of the railways in the Victorian era, speculation ran riot, with new suburbs fanning out from the strings of railway stations—first overground, then underground—to redraw the map of where and how people lived.

Throughout this expansion, London was one of the world's preeminent capitals of architecture, a city that ruled over an empire and had the bureaucratic, cultural, commercial, and spiritual monuments to prove it. After the tumult of World War II, during which around 60 percent of London's housing stock was destroyed by bombing, the city was ripe for reinvention. Yet many still believe that modern architecture has not been kind to a city with more than 2,000 years of history. Often deemed incongruous in scale or form, the vast state-sponsored building program that housed millions of people, usually substantially improving their amenity, nevertheless benefited the capital. However, it was commerce and economics that enabled the master builders and developers of the Georgian and Victorian eras to shape living conditions. In the modern era, it looked as if the capital's private housing would be redefined by the new emphasis on social motivation and material innovations. Ironically, by the start of the new century, it was apparent that—once again—the market would continue to shape the London house.

London's openness to modern architecture is one of the driving forces behind its gravity-defying property prices. In terms of culture and finance, London entered the twenty-first century as one of the world's most desirable destinations, whether for major financial institutions, foreign investors looking to speculate or cultural organizations wanting a high-profile base. London became associated with architectural one-liners that act as a visual shortcut for the city: the Gherkin (2003), the Walkie Talkie (2014), the Cheesegrater (2014), the Scalpel (2018), et al. Even the officially titled Shard (2012) understood the need for snappy branding. Eccentric skyscrapers notwithstanding, the city has also seen an infusion of major cultural projects over the past twenty years, kicked off by the opening of Herzog & de Meuron's Tate Modern in 2000 (extended in 2016) and including radical extensions or alterations to institutions such as the

British Museum, Victoria and Albert Museum, and Imperial War Museum. The capital's gallery scene has also proved another major driver for development, with projects including the White Cube in Bermondsey and Damien Hirst's Newport Street Gallery, an award-winning building by Caruso St. John, signaling a new maturity in design beyond the iconic form.

Where does this leave the private house? At the time of writing, with economic uncertainty back on the agenda, the steady rise in prices looks set to be tailing off, but not before it reached a peak far beyond the means of most ordinary Londoners. At the "super-prime" level—the industry word for properties "worth" in excess of £5 million—the cloud is fast eclipsing its silver lining, but not before a decade was spent reinvigorating the grand mansions of Chelsea, Kensington, and Mayfair with all the excessive accoutrements of modern living. Ironically, the city that abandoned its great legacy of social housing to the free market also looks set to be burdened with a surfeit of luxury apartments; it was reported in January 2018 that half of the luxury apartments built the previous year were still on the market.

It is against this backdrop that a new style of housing has begun to take root, one that defies the hyperbole of the real estate broker and

1 The Shard is Renzo Piano Building Workshop's bold and unmissable addition to the capital's twenty-first-century skyline. It remains the city's tallest building.
2 Georgian London is still highly sought after, both in terms of scale and quality. The Architectural Association School of Architecture is housed in Bedford Square, laid out in the late eighteenth century.

seeks out the most cost-effective sites, the most practical approaches to construction and ways in which buildings can be funded over decades by putting down proper roots. Unsurprisingly, London's population of architects has always been high, and many of the capital's small-scale developments are testament to this new way of thinking. The projects reproduced in this chapter all display this fusion of architecture and ingenuity, design and finance, pragmatism and pioneering approaches. Knox Bhavan and Chan + Eayrs both combined a speculative approach to design, while Kew House and Pear Tree House signify the perennial issue of land use, slotting elegant London dwellings into formerly neglected sites. There is still a place for trophy residential architecture—David Chipperfield in Knightsbridge, Shigeru Ban in Borough, Claudio Silvestrin in Hampstead—but the restrictions placed by planning and the sheer cost of building at scale often preclude architectural innovation in favor of a sleek, seductive "luxury modern" approach. London's housing issues will not go away overnight, but its conditions have encouraged a uniquely flexible and innovative approach to housing design that leaves no spaces undeveloped.

3 NEO Bankside, an award-winning apartment complex designed by Rogers Stirk Harbour and completed in 2012, epitomizes the modern luxury apartment building.
4 London's suburbs stretch out in every direction, and some enjoy spectacular views of the fast-changing city skyline.

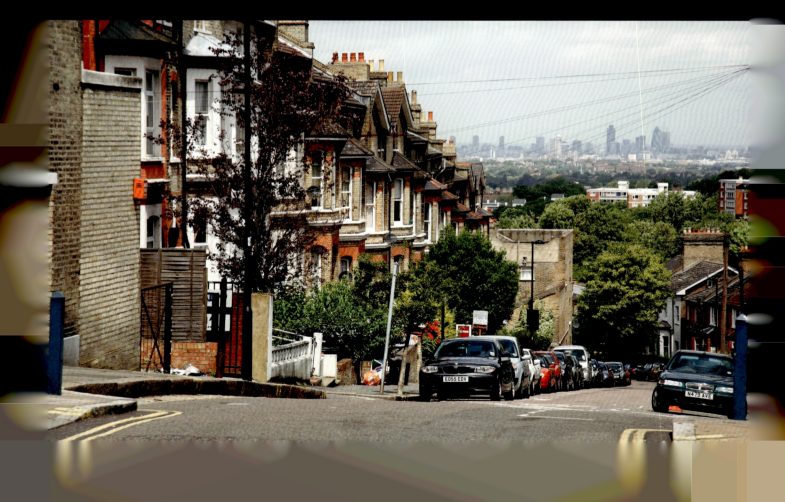

1   2

1 Zoe Chan poses outside her home and studio, Herringbone House in North London.   2 The project brings together Scandinavian aesthetics with elements of Chinese courtyard houses and Victorian references.

HERRINGBONE HOUSE

Tucked away behind a tall brick wall in North London, Herringbone House is a subtle fusion of styles and traditions. Densely populated and multicultural metropoles, such as London, are often the natural habitat for similar experiments that reflect the diversity and different perspectives of a varied and well-traveled population. Designed by Chan + Eayrs, a relatively young boutique studio founded by partners in work and life Zoe Chan and Merlin Eayrs, the house is the amalgamation of the pair's experiences, references, and tastes, and is inspired by traditional Chinese courtyard houses, Scandinavian simplicity, and Victorian architecture.

Set within a quiet residential street on the borders of Islington and Hackney, this project became reality when the architects spotted an opportunity for redevelopment—the site of a former car workshop—and decided to take it on to build their own home. The awkward-shaped plot is on a corner, wedged between rows of quaint

Victorian terraces. In order to protect the relatively low-rise structure from views in and to create a quiet haven for the residents, the architects hid the house behind the external wall's ornamental herringbone-patterned brickwork—a detail that came to define the project, and gave the house its name. Consequently, the part of the house that is visible from the street—an abstract outline of an archetypal house—does not reveal much, featuring only one long window on the first floor.

Behind the front wall unfolds a series of open rooms and courtyards that combine to compose a serene interior. Designed around a courtyard typology, the house includes a generous open-plan living space on the ground floor, which merges the lounge, kitchen, and dining areas that spill out effortlessly into two courtyards when the floor-to-ceiling sliding glass doors are open. A workspace also sits on one end of the ground level. The upper floor, accessed by an elegant

floating staircase, hosts the house's three light and airy bedrooms and a tumbled-marble off-white bathroom. At the same time, external shapes such as the house's gabled roof and use of brick are a nod to the surrounding terraces and nearby Gothic church, while the soft and natural palette of browns and creams underlines the atmosphere of a calm environment and references the couple's admiration for Nordic architecture. Walls and floors are lined in soaped, limed oak and tumbled Calacatta marble. Bespoke cabinetry and careful detailing make for an interior that feels both homely and polished.

Responding to its environment and site, Herringbone House is a modern interpretation of styles and periods that have been molded together into a neat, contemporary whole.

3 A slim floating staircase leads to the top floor, where the bedrooms are located.   4 Bespoke cabinetry and warm timber give this house its crisp look.   5 The living spaces include a sitting room and dining area, as well as a workspace.

LONDON
COUNTRY UK
ARCHITECT Knox Bhavan   **YEAR** 2014

1 The Brownstones are shaped to maximize the interior space.   2 An open-plan living area flows through each house.   3 Two houses are treated as one facade, a modern update of a long-standing vernacular approach.

LONDON BROWNSTONES

The London terraced house is an evolving architectural archetype that lends itself to almost infinite adaptation. Unsurprisingly, the past few decades have seen very little in the way of contemporary terraced housing built in the city, as a lack of sites, strict planning legislation, and the sheer cost of construction hamper new development.

Since Georgian times, the terrace has been the realm of the property speculator. In an Edwardian street in North Dulwich, a prosperous south London suburb, the entrepreneurial spirit is revived by a project that uses the terrace's harmonious proportions, space efficiency, and ongoing desirability to the best advantage. Architects Knox Bhavan, also based in south London, were commissioned by the client to design two new five-bedroom houses. The idea was for the client to live in one and to sell the other to fund the project, with the typology easing the case for planning and a mirrored floor plan simplifying the design. In the end, the houses differ subtly,

mainly due to the building line at the rear, which is cut back to preserve the rights to light of the adjoining street. A timber frame allowed for flexible construction, and while the houses synchronize effectively with their neighbors in terms of overall proportion and tone, the careful detailing is thoroughly contemporary.

Dubbed the "London Brownstones"—a nod to the ubiquitous terraced-housing style of New York — the houses are clad in terracotta sandstone with elements such as columns, lintels, and sills picked out in white sandstone. While not consistent with the level of decoration found in their Edwardian counterparts, the attention to detail is evident throughout, especially in terms of the use of simple materials such as brick, wood, polished concrete, and white plaster. At the rear, the "outrigger" is clad in tongue-and-groove larch boarding, and the internal joinery is especially well conceived throughout—another call back to the highly crafted nature of the original Victorian housing stock.

KEW HOUSE

Built in a conservation area near London's leafy Kew Gardens, this modern home was designed as an interpretation of the way in which a family wanted to live. Created in close collaboration between the architects, North London-based Piercy & Company, and their clients, Tim and Jo Lucas, Kew House sits on a plot behind a nineteenth-century stable wall, on a quiet residential street.

The house is split between two weathered steel gabled forms, conceived in order to break up the 3,960 square feet (368 sq m) of the structure's overall volume, and to remain in keeping with local massing according to planning regulations. This way, the design maintains a dialogue with the area's more vernacular forms. Limited access from only one side of the plot also heavily informed the design.

The clients wanted a home with ample space for activities, both for the adults and the children: a house that "delights." The architects obliged, creating a composition of rooms and clever features that more than satisfy the brief. There is a slide that leads to the basement from the first floor and a generous underground workshop. In addition, perforations on the steel skin, small and larger openings in unexpected places, and big windows ensure a strong connection between inside and outside.

In terms of volume composition, this house may appear sculptural and expressive at first glance, but its internal arrangement is in fact quite simple. The complex is composed of two rectangular wings, each spanning three levels, with one of the two wings being slightly set back from the street and sunken by 3 feet (1 m) below ground. They both have living spaces on the lower levels and bedrooms and bathrooms above. A glass circulation hall connects the two wings and allows ample light inside. Two courtyards sit on either side of the glass volume.

A softer, more contemporary interior in light tones and wood panels contrasts with the rustic metal exterior, with its pitched roofs and rougher surfaces. Finely crafted oak-veneer paneling and the extra-large planks of the Dinesen floors make for a streamlined interior that not only feels warm and natural, but also alludes to the

1 The striking Kew House combines a 19th-century stable wall with modern weathered steel forms.   2 The large family kitchen features floor-to-ceiling glazing that opens up to allow activities to spill out onto the courtyard.

owners' admiration for the Arts and Crafts Movement. Most of the bespoke joinery and cabinetwork, as well as the handrails, were CNC (computer numerical controlled) milled on site. The steel shells were prefabricated in Hull and then transported to London to be weathered outside in a yard.

Mixing traditional ideas and shapes with modern fabrication methods, Kew House is a four-bedroom family residence that plays with contrasts: rough and smooth, old and new, opaque and transparent. At the same time, the architects were mindful to keep the rooms carefully detailed but also informal, as this house was meant, first and foremost, to be a real family home.

3 Openings punched through in unexpected places create a variety of views and add an element of surprise. 4 Many of the house's bespoke parts were CNC cut on site.

1   2   3

1 Pear Tree House sits in a former Victorian orchard.   2 The house comprises two timber-clad volumes separated by a courtyard.   3 Inside, timber is matched by polished concrete floors for a sleek finish.

PEAR TREE HOUSE

Today, you would be hard pressed to find an empty plot of land to build on in London and, should you do so, prices are often prohibitive for the average household. So when prospective owners and their architects embark on a journey to design and build their own home, they often have to resort to creative solutions. Working with backyard plots and "hidden" sites is not uncommon; in fact, it is becoming the norm with regard to new builds in packed residential areas.

This is the route taken by architect Jake Edgley, when he began looking for the right plot to build his own family home. Upon discovering a backland lot around a 100-year-old pear tree in the remnants of what used to be a Victorian orchard in South London, Edgley knew he had come across the site of his future home. He planned the building around the existing tree, both to protect it and to use it to articulate open and closed areas in his design. The internal courtyard created around the tree brings light and air into the heart

of the house. This gesture also turns the house inward toward this open space and away from the surrounding terraced houses.

The linear floor plan follows the long and narrow site in a rather intuitive layout. Divided by the central courtyard into two distinct volumes, the house features a ground-level playroom and four bedrooms, including a generous master suite, above in the front wing, and open-plan living spaces topped by a guest room and study within the rear wing. The two parts of the house are linked by a glazed passage through the courtyard that acts as a bridge.

These two volumes are punctuated by further clearings and light wells, and are flanked by gardens at the front and back of the site. Planted roofs add extra greenery to the complex; you could easily forget that this house sits within one of the most populated capitals in the world. They also cleverly reduce visibility of the building from neighboring houses and, equally importantly, increase the project's

biodiversity, supporting existing local plant and animal life. Using tactile natural materials, Edgley sought to reference the site's historical use as an orchard by working with a vertical timber framework and wood finishes in both natural grains and a dark stained paneling effect. At the same time, smooth paving and polished concrete floors underline the house's contemporary character and minimalist interiors. Full-height, slim, gold trims around the windows and vent panels add an extra edge, but they also "break up the mass of these elevations," explain the architects, making this humble home not only considerate to its owner's needs, but also respectful of its neighbors and surrounding nature.

4 The courtyard is arranged around the house's namesake, a 100-year-old pear tree.   5 Vertical timber framework and metal details highlight the contemporary style of the interior.

PARIS

Modern Paris is still a city of apartment buildings. As set out in the nineteenth century under the auspices of Georges-Eugène Haussmann, the city was given a uniformity and grandeur that was to cement its center on an impressive scale, with broad avenues and boulevards, grand squares and parks, and an almost pathological aversion to the cramped, narrow streets and idiosyncratic houses that once formed the medieval city. Paris's radical reconstruction was social as well as architectural, with the new works intended to clear out working-class housing in favor of a new class of Parisian, with a carefully striated hierarchy that placed shop workers on the lower floors and the "upper classes" in grander apartments above them, away from the noise of the road. It stood to reason that the city's earliest modern structures were also apartment buildings, from Auguste Perret's prototypical concrete apartment block on Rue Franklin, which bridged the ornate world of nineteenth-century design and the rigour and simplicity of the twentieth century, to Robert Mallet-Stevens complex of houses and apartments on what is now, unsurprisingly, Rue Mallet-Stevens.

The city's architectural expression is a mix of grand uniformity and bold architectural gesture. The latter is exemplified by the two key symbols of Paris, then and now, the Arc de Triomphe (1836) and the Eiffel Tower (1889). They are both generators of urban form, major landmarks that not only orientate the pedestrian but also provide focal points about which the city revolves. Aside from the grand palais of the former nobility—re-purposed as official buildings, embassies, apartments, or galleries—there was little space in the modern Paris for private housing. The most significant experiments were characterized by their use of overlooked space, such as Pierre Chareau's Maison de Verre, one of the most remarkable private houses of the twentieth century. The Maison de Verre set the template for a whole new genre of architecture, one that favored industrial materials and components instead of traditional domestic-scale materials and spaces. It was hugely influential, as well as being rather atypical for the center of the city. There is a scattering of other key modernist buildings in the city itself, including Le Corbusier's Maison La Roche and Adolf Loos's house for the poet Tristan Tzara and his artist wife Greta Knutson. For the most part, though, the city center was stubbornly resistant to any deviation from Haussmann's style and ethos.

s suburbs. Here, in Meudon-Val-Fleury, you will find the house esigned at the end of the 1920s by Theo van Doesburg for his own se, and, in Poissy, the iconic white box of Le Corbusier's Villa Savoye, ompleted in 1931, as well as its late twentieth-century equivalent in aint-Cloud: the Villa dall'Ava, designed by Rem Koolhaas and ompleted in 1991. Such suburban villas did not speak much of the rban experience, but they served as experimental ventures in onstruction and formal arrangement. Consequently, innovation n French domestic architecture was largely focused on the partment and the suburb. Projects such as Jakob + MacFarlane's onnected House, completed in 2016, follow this pattern, drawing nspiration from both the suburban environment and the modernist recursors in the surrounding area.

For most people, their architectural experience of contemporary aris is defined by a surprisingly small number of truly significant uildings, from Richard Rogers and Renzo Piano's Pompidou Centre f 1977 through to the series of Grands Projets initiated by President rançois Mitterrand in the 1980s, which included galleries, a library, nd an opera house. Mitterrand was prescient, and realized that by ctively supporting large public buildings in the city he would ensure is own personal legacy. The results were some of the most iconic nd controversial structures of the era, in any country, predating the se of architectural "iconism" and even the deluge of projects that temmed from the United Kingdom's National Lottery windfall. They nclude Dominique Perrault's National Library of France, Jean Nouvel's rab World Institute, and Johan Otto von Spreckelsen's monumental a Grande Arche de la Défense. Taken together, these projects epresent the confidence of both the French state and the city itself, ven if individually many of them were considered to be over mbitious, over budget and prone to technical and design-driven nalfunctions. From a purely aesthetic point of view, Colin Fournier nd Bernard Tschumi's grandiose scheme for the landscape and tructures of the Parc de la Villette, a science-based visitor attraction nd public space occupying the city's vast former abattoirs and meat narket, was probably the most successful. Attracting attention efore it was even finished, the Parc de la Villette was perhaps the nest example of the architecture of Deconstructivism, a niche form f philosophy that embodied the disassociation between form and unction, tradition and history. Tschumi scattered a grid of red amed pavilions across the site, a series of thirty-five architectural ollies" that followed a broadly domestic architecture scale. They gnified the quandaries at the heart of French architecture: that f the relationship between elaborate form and simple function, etween social utility and bourgeois enjoyment.

Paris continued to compartmentalize its housing, albeit not on ich an explicit scale as Haussmann. In the 1960s and 1970s, great

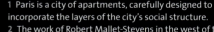

1 Paris is a city of apartments, carefully designed to incorporate the layers of the city's social structure.
2 The work of Robert Mallet-Stevens in the west of the city is a rare example of this talented architect's urban contribution combining different-scaled forms and structures with a unifying aesthetic .

swathes of the *banlieues* (suburbs) were redeveloped as high-rise estates, effectively creating an even starker social divide than the one that existed in the nineteenth century. Despite a formal inventiveness and idiosyncratic approach that was almost entirely absent in other mass housing projects, contemporary architecture was ultimately discredited as inhumane and banal.

Today, Paris has not lost its penchant for big works, but the country's architectural identity has evolved considerably over the past few decades. This has taken the form of renovations, reconstructions, and new-build houses that eschew the formality of style in favor of a more pragmatic, *ad hoc* approach to design. Overshadowed for so long by the weight of history—and the even more crushing weight of heroic modernism—the greater Paris area is once again home to housing innovation.

Villette, an enormous urban park built on the site of the city's slaughterhouses. The planning was overseen by Bernard Tschumi in the 1980s. **4** The Maison de Verre, designed by Pierre Chareau between 1928 and 1932, is a prototypical modern urban dwelling, elegant but prosaic in its use of technology and available space.

1 This suburban Parisian house is the renovation and extension of a modest existing home.   2 Referencing the area's double pitched roofs, the architects created a timber-clad upper level volume that juts out.

ECO-DURABLE BOIS TYPE II

Paris-based architecture firm Djuric Tardio, founded in 2004 by Mirco Tardio and Caroline Djuric, specializes in urban residential projects with a sustainability twist. Their desire to experiment and research forms of eco-friendly building has led the pair to create a number of environmentally considerate, modern townhouses, such as their flagship Eco-Durable Bois Type I renovation project from 2014. A year later, the practice's second investigation into building sustainably with wood within an urban context resulted in a new single-family house in Issy-les-Moulineaux, a relatively densely built neighborhood in the southwestern suburbs of Paris.

The project, a commission for the renovation and extension of an existing home, is set within a residential area made up of an eclectic mix of different building scales and styles, from existing twentieth-century private houses to more contemporary, larger, multifamily housing of several floors. Working with a building that is already a few decades old and sits within an established streetscape, the architects decided to follow the area's existing architectural language and to create a house with a double pitched roof, which referenced some of the local vernacular. The team opted for a timber construction, but one that would comfortably fit within a modern design and the structure's clean outline and minimalist aesthetic. Boosting the house's overall surface was a key requirement of their brief, so from the street's side, the timber structure juts out by some 4 feet (1.25 m). This overhang creates a semi-open space that welcomes visitors by protecting them under an entrance canopy, but also considerably increases the house's floor area upstairs. At the same time, this gesture puts the focus on the top floor, which, combined with the simple glazed ground level, creates a sense of lightness.

In total, the house spans a relatively generous 1, 938 square feet (180 sq m) across three floors. The lower levels are built on the

3 The ground level is taken over by the house's generous living spaces. **4** The lounge opens up toward a back garden through a fully glazed facade that bathes the interior with sunlight.

original structure's existing walls, but the upper levels and roof are entirely new. At ground level, there is a generous reception and dining area, with a separate kitchen on one side and a living space on the other, set in a conservatory overlooking the garden. Four bedrooms, a bathroom, and a separate toilet sit under the structure's pitched timber roof and open up to a terrace on the garden's side. This offers ample outdoor space under a pergola. The overhang at the front provides parking spots for the two family cars, while a staircase at the back leads down to the cellar.

The timber cladding wrapping around the house's main volume not only gives it its distinct look, but also acts as horizontal sun shading, protecting the fully glazed living spaces behind it from the region's occasionally intense summer heat. In order to further protect the house from energy loss and to optimize thermal performance, the architects updated the existing lower levels' insulation to modern standards. Mixing old and new, and combining timber, steel, and concrete, this experimental house shows how old structures can evolve, adapt, and ultimately be reborn for the twenty-first century.

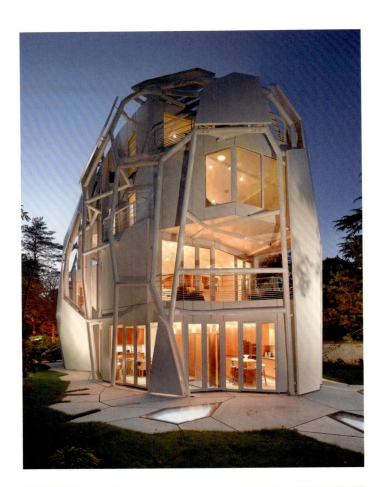

PARIS
COUNTRY France
ARCHITECT Jakob + MacFarlane   YEAR 2016

MAISON CONNECTÉE

Set in the affluent wooded suburb of Boulogne-Billancourt in Paris, this spectacular villa pays homage to the architectural experimentation of its immediate neighbors, while also remaining utterly contemporary. The work of the Paris-based architectural firm Jakob + MacFarlane, the Connected House was delivered to an exacting brief, reflecting the needs of clients who had a lifetime of object collecting and books to display. While the furnishings and artworks are eclectic, the dual exterior skins of this four-story structure peel back to reveal a layer within.

Clad in white enamelled aluminum panels, the house is built around a tubular steel frame, which then forms an exoskeleton on top of the first layer of cladding. A second, faceted outer skin—described as "bark" by the architects—gives form to the house, creating an organic structure that appears to bloom out of the ground in its suburban site. The architects refer to several earlier precedents in the area, including work by Robert Mallet-Stevens and Le Corbusier, thereby setting the scene for grand villas that epitomize the structure, style, and approach of their era. Maison Connectée (Connected House) is certainly well appointed, with a basement pool and rooftop terrace.

The structure is the connecting element referenced in the name, branching out with bark-like cladding. Jakob + MacFarlane is well-known for its extensive use of geometric forms, and Maison Connectée runs with its tree metaphor throughout: the "branches" support the internal floors and a central circulation core serves as a trunk, rising up from the basement to the top-floor terrace. The stair tower also includes a series of bespoke French oak bookcases and two custom-made aquariums. The environmental impact of the house has been minimized by the use of clever engineering, including ground water-sourced heating and energy as well as an extensive home automation system.

1 The house is contained by steel structural "trees."   2 The structure is exposed internally.   3 An external staircase leads to the terrace.   4 The steel elements frame the view. Overleaf The living room has custom-made cabinetry.

MAISON ESCALIER

Finding empty plots and new-build houses in the heart of historical Paris is rare, yet Maison Escalier sits nestled within the 6th arrondissement, occupying a space between two existing buildings on a well-preserved block. The architect behind it, Paris-based Jacques Moussafir, envisioned this house "as a tree-like structure," he explains.

Defined by the three walls that surround it, which have been painted white, Maison Escalier expands across several wood-veneered floors. The new dark timber elements—floors, ceilings, walls, and cabinetry—sit in contrast to the existing whitewashed rough brick walls in a gesture that clearly defines what is new and what is not. While the north and east facades had to be preserved in order to comply with local planning regulations, the south facade is where the architecture comes into its own. Moussafir created an entirely glazed frontage, theatrically clad in steel, that allows glimpses of the interior through a densely perforated pattern. Its articulation into different volumes also hints at the volumetric complexity of the interior spaces behind it.

Designed almost as one single giant staircase, the house breaks internally into five half-levels, linked by generous stairs. There is a cinema room in the basement, a living, kitchen, and dining floor above, a study area a few steps up from there, a bedroom level, and a roof terrace at the very top. Cleverly built-in storage, from cabinets to shelves and hidden closets, lines the timber-clad sides, thus ensuring that the interior remains sleek, uncluttered and flexible. The constant change in levels between functions means that very few walls are necessary in this house. Areas that require more privacy, such as the wet room, are built within the central staircase's core—the "tree's" trunk—and the stair's landings effectively become the house's "rooms."

The relatively compact 1,615-square-foot (150 sq m) structure is made of steel, with the floors cantilevered out of the central core.

1 An intricate perforated steel screen covers the front facade, in a pattern that references foliage.   2 Inside, floors are cantilevered off a central core.   3 Dark wood and hidden storage ensure the interiors remain sleek and uncluttered.

As the house is tucked away beside existing taller buildings, Moussafir cut two light wells on the northeast and northwest corners of the house. These ensure that plenty of light penetrates all areas, while the residents can catch views of the sky from almost anywhere inside.

Experiencing Maison Escalier is a joy: internal movement has a distinct flow, leading visitors up and down the sculptural staircases, through the smooth, chocolate timber-wrapped interiors and guiding them to openings, either up, across or out through the laser-cut, leaf-motif steel skin. The patterns make the structure glow at night, while creating a dynamic play of shadows inside.

4   5

4 Maison Escalier's clever level changes mean that very few walls are needed to define the rooms.   5 The staircase landings expand to form the different floors.

ROTTERDAM

COUNTRY Netherlands
ARCHITECT MVRDV **YEAR** 2016

1 The street facade is a rigorous brick box, broken only by the entrance hall. 2 The interior curves around an existing tree. 3 A balcony follows the curve of the top floor. 4 Service areas are hidden behind wooden panels.

CASA KWANTES

Casa Kwantes is a house of two parts, its two facades offering up very different views on the world. Situated in the west of Rotterdam, in a dense slice of suburban landscape, the house occupies a corner plot that was previously the site of an old hospital. Surrounding houses are mostly brick and neo-vernacular, but MVRDV's new house is decidedly different. The mysterious rectangular facade has minimal detailing and openings and is finished in the uniform texture created by a light, slim, engineering brick. Celosías (latticework) panels allow in light, but prevent prying eyes.

Access to the property is via a curved indentation in the facade, which takes the visitor into a dark entrance hall. Without warning, the house suddenly inverts its approach and switches priorities, opening up to a glazed garden facade formed with a swooping "U" shape of two stories of floor-to-ceiling curved glass. A ribbon of frameless glass balcony runs the full length of this elevation,

mirroring the path of the walls, while an ancient olive tree takes pride of place on the stone terrace. Daylight and open-living spaces are balanced with seclusion and privacy.

Casa Kwantes draws visual inspiration from high Dutch modernism, not only in the use of precisely tailored brick but also in the spirited swoops and curves of the glass facade. At 5,165 square feet (480 sq m), it is generously sized and also accommodates a double garage. The ground floor is kept almost entirely open plan, with the services, storage, and functions set behind a long wall of elegant wooden paneling that is aligned with the straight-edged street facade. This set-up allows for two living/dining spaces that reach out into the garden, as well as a library area, all finished with the same continuous stone flooring.

The first floor contains three bedrooms, two in one "wing" and a master suite in the other, united by the long shared balcony. A small

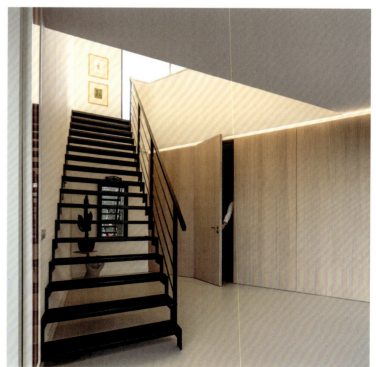

basement provides extra storage, while the flat roof is home to a large solar array. Solar gain helps heat the space in the winter and the first-floor balcony provides shading in the summer months. With the help of a ground source heat pump, the house generates enough energy to mitigate for the large glazed walls and be almost entirely self sufficient. Despite its discreet roadside appearance and sustainable credentials, Casa Kwantes stands out in its conservative environs. The architects worked hand in hand with their clients to deliver a tailor-made home, but many negotiations were needed with the local municipality to get the design approved.

5 Enormous panels of curved glass open up the house to the garden.   6 The open-plan ground floor is contrasted with a more conventional upstairs plan.

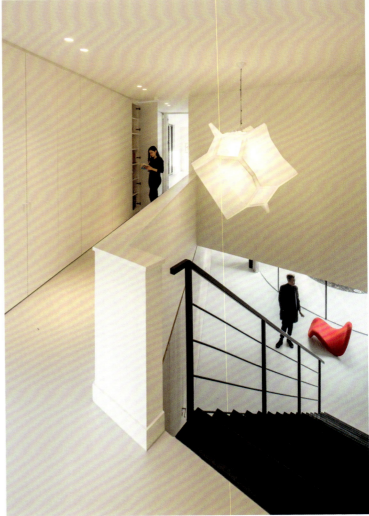

1 The owner collaborated with fellow architect Bruno Vanbesien on the design.   2 The main living areas are on the first floor.   3 These glass doors can open fully, allowing the owner to sleep underneath the stars.

HOUSE CM

This new-build house in the small Belgian town of Zellik, a short drive from Brussels, appears modest in size, seemingly spanning only two floors and slotted discreetly between its twentieth-century neighbors. However, its timber-paneled facade is deceptive. Designed by Bruno Vanbesien in collaboration with Christophe Meersman—the latter of whom is both an architect and the owner of the house—House CM has more to offer than meets the eye.

Camouflaging the house's true nature, the external paneling—made out of tropical hardwood—decorates the volume, running all the way up the front and over the top, covering the roof and back of the house like a sinuous skin. It also creates, in a single gesture, a unified design approach that reveals little of what is going on behind the walls of House CM. The architects opted for a deliberately ambiguous design, in order to create an element of surprise and mystery. A large full-width opening sits across the front facade, between the ground

and first floors. This allows for light to flood in, but also ensures privacy and a sense of separation from the street.

The back of the house is a different story. Flexible and transparent, the rear facade is expressive and open, looking out toward the property's garden. The glass panels can be drawn back so that inside and outside can merge in the pleasantly warm summer days. The line between indoors and outdoors is blurred, both visually, through the glass walls, and physically. On the second floor, one of the bedrooms holds a small surprise: its floor-to-ceiling glass terrace doors can open fully, allowing the bed to be rolled out so that the owner can sleep under the stars. Cool, natural-stone floors and basalt tiles inside accentuate this connection between indoors and outdoors.

The house spans four levels, connected by a floating metal staircase. A parking garage is accessible from the street on the ground floor; the first floor is the main entertainment space, including

4 The minimalist interior combines dark wood with white walls and cabinetry.   **5** This timber-clad structure's facade includes a large opening that permits a glimpse inside.

kitchen, dining, and sitting areas; bedrooms and bathrooms are located on the second floor, while the smaller top level is reserved for a study area.

The elegant metal staircase, with its glazed landings, acts as the house's main circulation core. Its light construction was designed to make it slender and discreet, in order to allow in as much natural light as possible through the skylight at the top. At the same time, the staircase matches the overall structure's minimalist interior.

Working with a familiar residential typology—the humble row townhouse—in an unassuming city street, Vanbesien and Meersman created a structure that is full of surprises, from its enigmatic skin and many outdoor areas, to its unexpected large openings at the back that make the house glow like a lantern at night.

HOUSE Z

A suburban house with a truly urban view, Bayer & Strobel's House Z is situated in a Frankfurt suburb, raised up above the nearby city center to give its residents a spectacular view of the distant skyline above the trees from the upper levels. The Kaiserslautern-based architects designed House Z around this privileged vantage point. Brick built, with a deep recessed terrace, large windows, and patterns set into the brickwork of the ground floor walls to bring plenty of light flooding into the interior, the house makes a strong sculptural statement on its hillside location.

Frankfurt's many suburbs have a wide diversity of architectural forms. Germany's historic low rates of outright home ownership mean that truly individual statements are relatively rare and grand statement homes are not as prevalent as they are in other urban and suburban locations around Europe. In Germany, the modern house, where it exists, tends to be up to date and flexible, but with a modest use of materials and a desire not to stand out.

In the design of House Z, the architects inverted the traditional single-family floor plan to give prominence to the views. Bedrooms are placed on the lower stories, while the living areas are located on the top floor, where the best view can be found at the family dining table. A terrace at ground-floor level bisects the building, with a top-lit staircase in the center of the house stepping down to a basement, where there is an annex, and leading up to the main living space. An entrance hall and garage are also on the ground floor.

The facade is finished throughout in clinker masonry, a high-heat process that results in harder, more durable, but also less uniform bricks than conventional firing. The effect is of a solid volume with punched carved forms within it, almost geological in its appearance. Inside and out, all the finishes are durable and hard wearing—plastered white walls, built-in furniture, and natural stone floors, for example—but the careful composition and detailing give the house a refined, luxurious feel. "Rather than echoing short-lived trends, the design is committed to a contemporary but enduring architectural language," the architects say.

1 The garden facade is defined by the recessed terrace and patterned brick screens.   2 Light gray-beige stones form the clinker masonry.   3 Bold pattern is also used internally.   4 Light is directed down the main staircase.

HOUSE B

Along the Swiss lakes' idyllic coast, urban and suburban unite, with smaller villages merging and becoming part of a continuous suburb of the larger cities in the region, such as Lausanne, Geneva, and Zurich. This sculptural house on Lake Zurich's Gold Coast is part of such a landscape. Created by local architects E2A, headed by brothers Piet and Wim Eckert, House B is an architectural exercise in its particular typology and an apt case study representing the Swiss suburban realm.

Sitting in a context of pitched roofs, conventional architectural styles, and green spaces (mostly former agricultural zones that have been preserved by planning regulations, to ensure the urban fabric does not get too dense), the house is located within a quiet residential area of row housing and domestic gardens. However, it clearly stands out among its neighbors for its rough, board-formed concrete volumes and hard edges. A perimeter of walls and hedges circles a private enclosed space of refuge for the residents. Designed to have this clear border, the house "reflects on this relationship between the inside and the outside," explain the architects. So, while the structure's exterior seems hard and impenetrable, the interior has been designed in a "softer" style, featuring bright, open rooms and planted clearings, in the shape of an entry court and a garden.

Inside, the structure leads the visitor through an entrance lobby and up to the first floor via the house's main circulation core. This level hosts the living spaces and includes a centrally located kitchen and dining room, as well as an impressive double-height sitting room. A terrace on this level looks out toward the lake and mountains beyond, while a separate staircase connects with the garden below. The top floor houses the master suite and an office space. Large openings and internal balconies allow views out; at the same time, their positioning is such that views in are limited, thus guaranteeing privacy for the residents.

This is not just a sleek, minimalist home; it is also a modern refuge that has been designed to shut out the world and provide a sanctuary for its residents, while at the same time discreetly opening up toward the beautiful Swiss nature that surrounds it.

1 The house is a sculptural composition of open and closed planes.
2 The mezzanine enjoys idyllic views.   3 A terrace acts as a lookout point.   4 A walled perimeter conceals a small garden.
Overleaf House B is made up of simple geometric forms.

COUNTRY Portugal
ARCHITECT Pablo Pita   YEAR 2016

CASA BOAVISTA

Located in the heart of Porto, on the celebrated street that also gives its name to the city's football team, Casa Boavista is a radical house refurbishment in a historic cityscape. The original site was little more than a ruined shell at the end of a terrace of similar surviving structures. On the other side, there was a taller building, offering the potential for a roof extension.

Pablo Pita, a studio set up in Porto by Pablo Rebelo and Pedro Pita, decided to preserve the original stonework, retaining it as a minimal framework around which they inserted the new Casa Boavista. Their additions include a new floor and a new garage, even though the site is relatively narrow. At the rear, the house still retains its generous rear garden. The ground-floor entrance hallway runs alongside the garage, leading past the towering internal atrium to a generous extended living and dining space at the rear of the house, which opens out into the stone-walled garden. Like many traditional houses in the region, the ground floor has large sliding wooden shutters that serve to open up the whole space to the outside or keep it shaded and private. Shutters are also used elsewhere in the project, both inside and out, not only for privacy but also to increase the feeling of solid volumes throughout the house.

At the center of Casa Boavista, the atrium forms a top-lit core that rises the full height of the property. On the upper two floors there are three bedrooms and an office, with rear-facing terraces on each level. A large, frameless skylight brings sunlight down into the heart of the house, creating the impression of an entirely open internal courtyard, a feeling enhanced by the inclusion of shutters on the internal windows. The resulting space is on a scale that evokes a traditional narrow residential courtyard; it also provides views across and between floors to increase the sense of distance and space within the house. In stark contrast, the rear facade makes the different levels and new additions far more explicit, with alternate

1   2

1 The rear elevation shows the additional floors and different material treatments.   2 The kitchen can be shielded from the sun by a series of large sliding wooden screens.

bands of white and dark finishes on the walls. On the top floor, the two uppermost bedrooms are extended up into the pitch of the roof with a design that makes the most of the relatively small footprint of the original house.

Materials are kept simple throughout and include polished wood floors, solid wooden stair treads and shutters, and white plastered walls, as well as gloss-white kitchen cabinets to bounce light in from the rear glazing. There are hints of industrial design with the solid concrete shelf in the living space and the all-concrete bathroom, a dark and atmospheric space that provides a stark contrast to the otherwise regular palette, enhancing the feeling of a house with its own internal private landscape, tucked away in the heart of the city.

BARCELONA
COUNTRY Spain
ARCHITECT Alventosa Morell   YEAR 2014

CASA CP

Barcelona's most prevalent form of housing is the apartment building. In the nineteenth century, the city was laid out as a grid by the pioneering urban planner Ildefons Cerdà, who demolished the *ad hoc* street arrangement within the old city walls in favor of a unifying grid pattern, complete with set-back facades at crossroads and grand boulevards. Contemporary private houses such as Casa CP are relatively rare. This new private house by Alventosa Morell Arquitectes is certainly familiar with the city's prevailing conditions, for it is sandwiched between two apartment buildings. The architects' brief was to make the most of this potentially overbearing situation without losing the most important qualities of urban living: quiet space and natural light. In addition to the confined setting, noise from traffic was a major issue.

Alventosa Morell Arquitectes set out to minimize these two downsides and transform them into a positive. Consequently, the house is divided into two zones, with the "night zone" nearest the street and living spaces orientated toward the inside of the block. The house is set over four stories—three of which are above ground—with a roof terrace on the upper floor. As a result, the street facade is refined and simple, hinting at very little of what happens behind it. Less domestic in massing and materials than its apartment building neighbors, Casa CP is defined by an extensive use of wood, with the different floor levels clearly defined and two recessed balconies for the bedrooms.

From the street, Casa CP appears like a piece of urban furniture, a cabinet for city living with compartments that can be revealed depending on the seasons, the time of day, and the needs and moods of the occupants. Although it is domestic in scale, the absence of regularly proportioned doors and windows gives little clue as to the scope and identity of the house, allowing it to effectively fade anonymously into the streetscape.

The rear facade is, by contrast, much more open and transparent, bringing light into the heart of this long, narrow 55-foot (17 m) site plan. A small courtyard terrace at first-floor level is surrounded by

1 The slender staircase is a precise combination of painted steel and wood.   2 The rear of the house is tightly knitted into the urban context, with slatted screens for privacy.   3 The front facade is a carefully controlled composition of steel and wood.

high walls, thus allowing the living space to flow from inside out without increasing the chance of being overlooked. Natural light is also brought deep into the plan via a series of folding shutters, blinds, and skylights.

The stairwell is made of slender white-painted steel, with open wooden treads to maximize the penetration of light from the upper levels downward. This minimal treatment extends to the balustrade designs, while the rest of the house is also pared back. The detailing includes an absence of skirtings and decoration, allowing the carefully aligned floor and wall planes to be consistently finished in a single material, greatly adding to the sense of space. The end result is an inward-looking urban oasis, one that shelters its occupants from the city outside while selectively bringing in light and views.

4 The rear screens act as a second skin in front of sliding glass doors.   5 The kitchen is arranged as a long galley, deep in the plan.   6 Splashes of colored tiles are used in the bathrooms.

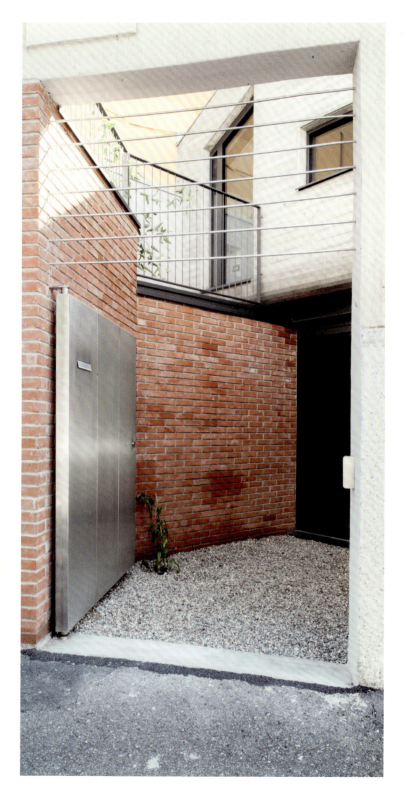

1 UV House is set behind a small faceted courtyard.
2 A private terrace is reached by a folded steel stair.
3 Another folded steel internal stair unites the open-plan space. **Overleaf** The kitchen overlooks the outdoor area.

UV HOUSE

From the street, UV House is almost invisible. A classic infill site, the project started out as a light industrial building: long, thin, land-locked and top lit. The opportunity to turn it into a private house for a young couple demanded a careful subdivision of the space to maintain outdoor areas and impressive interior volumes.

Pietro Ferrario and Francesco Enea Castellanza of OASI architects decided to insert a sleeping mezzanine inside the existing space. Formed of poured concrete, the floating slab curves round to make a facade, ceiling, and balustrade, thereby creating a uniform textured surface throughout the house. From the patio garden at the front, the new concrete facade appears to rest atop the brick walls, with the curved detailing at the base of the wall giving it an independent feel. Two bedrooms and bathrooms are located on the upper floor in this new addition, set beneath a wooden roof and reached from an internal staircase. The stairwell is also the main living space, a

double-height area that preserves the original height of the old building, with hard-wearing flooring evoking its initial industrial purpose. A private roof terrace is accessed from the second bedroom, with an external stairway leading down to a triangular brick-lined entrance courtyard.

Space is tight, but the use of minimal detailing and uniform materials for walls and floors—with the occasional flash of restored original brickwork—gives the house a pared-back, gallery-like feel. The steel staircase is especially well detailed, intersecting with the poured-concrete sleeping area and the ground floor. The external metal stair is similarly straightforward, and balustrades and windows all have a simple industrial aesthetic. In addition, the open-plan living space has a wall of glass that leads onto the patio garden, creating an airy, open feel that is at odds with UV House's discreet location in a northern Italian city.

PETRALONA HOUSE

In the heart of contemporary Athens's sea of concrete and polykatoikies—the typical large-scale multifamily housing seen in Greek urban centers—finding the space to create a new single-family home can seem like a luxury, and it is certainly a rarity. The country's rapid urbanization during the second half of the twentieth century has led to densely packed city centers, and nowhere is this more evident than in the Greek capital. However, there are still some pockets of lower-scale neighborhoods to be found, and Petralona, one of the popular Athenian districts that sit at the foot of Mount Filopappou, is one of them.

This is where local architecture practice Point Supreme, headed by partners in work and life Konstantinos Pantazis and Marianna Rentzou, built this house, which is the pair's own family home and studio. At first glance, its overall shape and concrete construction may not seem miles away from the area's traditional single dwellings, but upon closer inspection a number of unexpected spaces and little surprises start to unfold. Petralona House is, the architects explain, many houses combined into one.

The structure is divided into three main horizontal zones. The ground level is closely linked to nature, opening up through large panels of glazing toward the garden at the back; a winter garden and indoor tree take this connection with nature even further. This is where the triple-height, open-plan kitchen, dining and living room is located, along with a guest space. The first floor, which houses the master bedroom and a bathroom, has a more informal, folk-inspired feel, featuring traditional awning and detailing that references Cycladic island architecture. A side door leads out to a generous terrace that expands over the living spaces underneath. There, a concrete bench is strategically orientated toward a large mural, designed by the architects and inspired by ancient Greek urns. The top level hosts the workspaces and has a distinct minimalist feel,

1 A mural, created by the architects, can be admired from the terrace.   2 A planted tree within the triple-height living space highlights the connection to the outdoors.   3 Large windows and glass doors lead out to a small garden.

being consciously pared down and featuring little color and ornamentation. It is also slightly set back from the street, creating a narrow terrace.

Using traditional techniques and materials as well as reclaimed and found objects, the pair created a house full of surprises and different textures. Its vibrant color combinations are a joy, and sophisticated craftsmanship, such as the staircase's metalwork, shows that this is not a piece of work that the architects took on lightly. Sponsored materials and finishes, such as the plugs, tiles, and bathroom furniture, reflect the idea of a "collage," which was one of the key concepts — not because of a random architectural fancy, but in order to create the carefully planned narrative that unfolds when walking through the different spaces. Analogue systems and manual mechanisms, such as the controlling of the temperature and openings, ensure that the residents remain in touch with the physicality of the structure. A set of stairs on the front facade's top balcony leads up to the roof terrace, where an unexpected view of the Acropolis completes the journey through this delightful composition.

4 The house's theatricality unfolds in the living space. 5 Traditional shutters and tiles hint at local building materials and techniques. 6 An open-plan kitchen sits next to the dining and living room.

MOSCOW

COUNTRY Russia
ARCHITECT Zaha Hadid Architects   YEAR Ongoing

1 The architect's signature curvy futuristic lines are visible both inside and out in these digital renders.   2 A whole floor is dedicated to the living and entertaining rooms. Overleaf The tower serves as a lookout platform.

CAPITAL HILL RESIDENCE

Russia's capital features a center filled with grand public buildings, colorful churches and beautiful monuments, plus a series of outer urban rings made up from large-scale concrete residential blocks that house a large proportion of the city's 12 million or so citizens. Farther out are the uber suburbs, full of great leafy patches and luxurious dachas, with many so big that they blur the boundaries between suburban and rural. The Capital Hill Residence sits in such a part of Moscow's outskirts, on a hillside within the small community of Barvikha. The site's natural scenery is striking; tall trees, mostly pine and birch, form the beginnings of a rich, dark forest.

When Zaha Hadid Architects were called upon to build a villa here for a local client, they knew they had to make the most of this stunning landscape, which is how this project's distinctive massing arrangement was born. The house is composed of two parts. One is strategically merged within the plot's topography, following the

natural slope and kept relatively low and organic in shape. The second rises straight up and floats elegantly some 72 feet (22 m) above the ground, as a kind of contemporary lookout tower. Internally, the villa spreads across four levels. From the basement up it includes a leisure zone, with massage room, fitness areas, sauna, and hammam; a main living space, with dining, kitchen, and entertainment areas as well as a pool; a first floor that houses the entrance lobby, study, library, guest room, and children's room; and at the top is the generous master suite and lounge, looking out over the treetops from its large terrace.

Zaha Hadid Architects' sinuous design creates a flowing space, lit beautifully from skylights in the main double-height living areas. The practice's signature curvaceous concrete forms are complemented by swathes of glass and steel, creating a smooth narrative when moving from one space to the next. Strategically placed floor-to-ceiling openings frame the forest beyond.

AFRICA

CASABLANCA LAMU ISLAND
CAPE TOWN

2 This old, faded, Portuguese colonial villa is located in the town of Inhambane, Mozambique.

It is difficult to do justice to the sheer variety of Africa's contemporary architecture. There is no overarching point of focus to explore change on the continent, unlike the ideological and industrial revolution in Asia, for example. The African experience is also vastly different from country to country, north to south, ocean to ocean, and there are no simple narratives for the way architecture is perceived, practiced, and progressed.

This chapter focuses on just a few projects from a small proportion of Africa's fifty-four countries, a sampling too small to provide even a snapshot of trends and debates. Instead, what these case studies reveal is that the preoccupations and approaches in Africa have much in common with building design the world over: namely, architecture can be used to improve the quality of life through space, economics, and technology.

Africa has a rapidly urbanizing population. Today, there are many fast-growing urban areas, including Cairo, Johannesburg, Nairobi, Lagos, Accra in Ghana, Khartoum in the Sudan, and Kinshasa in the Democratic Republic of Congo. Of these, only Cairo, Lagos, and Kinshasa are defined as megacities, with populations in excess of 10 million. Projections suggest that by 2030 these cities will have doubled in size, with Lagos becoming Africa's most populous city. By mid-century, half of the continent's estimated population of 2 billion will live in urban areas. Declining child mortality, lengthening life spans and improving economies will need to be countered by vastly improved infrastructure. But just as the China of today provides a benchmark for how populous countries can facilitate major cultural shifts in the use of renewable technology, for example, there are many opportunities ahead.

The challenges are also numerous. For a long time, "Africa" was a case study, a demonstration of how complex systems could arise out of apparent chaos. The most prominent of these studies was Rem Koolhaas's focus on Lagos in Nigeria. For Koolhaas, an architect and social theorist best known for the work of his practice OMA, Lagos was an object lesson in opportunity, a self-organizing system that showcases the ingenuity and resilience of the human condition. It was an optimistic reading, one that critics noted was easy to make from a distance. "As a picture of the urban future, Lagos is fascinating only if you're able to leave it," George Packer noted drily in *The New Yorker* (The Megacity, November 13, 2006). "After just a few days in the city's slums, it is hard to maintain Koolhaas's intellectual excitement. What he calls 'self-organization' is simply collective adaptation to extreme hardship." For his part, Koolhaas responded to the "innuendo" by winding down his projects in the city, although they were later rekindled, saying that Packer's comments were "the first manifestation of what is currently a really big issue: how political correctness defines the limits of what you can do."

The controversy highlights one of the key problems of writing about design in Africa. The extremities are so extreme, and the variety so diverse, that to highlight one particular element risks excluding a thousand more. A city like Lagos has long been distorted by Nigeria's oil wealth, the vast majority of which does not get fed back into the country's infrastructure but is siphoned off by a small percentage of the population (and foreign businesses). Such disparities are all too common in a continent rich in natural resources, and as a result it is not surprising to find similar disparities in the way people live. The townships of South Africa sit in uneasy proximity to the gated communities of the new middle classes, while the country's wilder shores are crowded with the kind of generic upscale international modernism found in moneyed communities around the world. Modern architecture is about wealth, not equality.

There are prominent examples of projects that buck the trend. Investment in infrastructure is the most convincing way of ridding a megacity of its slums, but the mechanics and politics of creating and supplying proper utilities go far beyond the scope of this book. Instead, design is a sticking plaster of good intentions, a way of using existing conditions and methods to make things better, without the scope and ability to start again. This is not to equate the conditions or cultures found in one country and the next, but simply to acknowledge that it is local conditions, above all, that must be considered at the root of every project.

There are some fine examples of early modern architecture around Africa, in places as diverse as Ethiopia, Nigeria, and the former Commonwealth. But to the modern eye, this is yet another manifestation of colonialism, an imposition that had little to do with local conditions and everything to do with the paternalistic attitude of the West. Maxwell Fry and Jane Drew's *Tropical Architecture in the Dry and Humid Zones* (1956) was typical of the era, a celebration of the "civilizing" effects of modern architecture, concerned with improved conditions, of course, but also how the aesthetics of vernacular design might come to be absorbed and accommodated by new, mostly concrete, architecture. Even after the independence movement of the 1950s and 1960s, many of the most dramatic buildings created to define these brand new nations were in fact designed by Western architects, only too happy to showboat for a fresh set of newly moneyed clients.

Modern sensibilities are more sensitive and accommodating, yet "African design" is still an unnecessarily broad term to cover what is a necessarily broad range of work. A Moroccan or Kenyan townhouse might evoke the spirit and forms of societies that have existed for hundreds of years, but they are entirely different from a modular design for housing in Cape Town, designed not only to work with dense site conditions but also the available financing and need for flexible uses. Kunlé Adeyemi's most high-profile work in Nigeria is explicitly designed for communities that exist outside conventional urbanism. His Makoko Floating School was rebuilt for display at the 2016 Venice Biennale, although the original was subsequently destroyed in a storm on the Lagos Lagoon. In comparison, there is the work of La Voûte Nubienne, a French NGO dedicated to exploring the vernacular architecture of the Sudan, in particular the "Nubian vault," traditionally formed from mudbrick. Are any of these projects more African than the other? Any analysis of contemporary African architecture is a timely reminder of the need to become more accepting of pluralism and more attuned to inequality.

VILLA AGAVA

The traditional housing type in Morocco, as with many other North African countries, is based around an internal courtyard, often with high walls around any perimeter space and screens to provide both privacy and shading. Built on a tight plot surrounded by neighboring properties in the Moroccan city of Casablanca, Villa Agava does not have a central open space, but it does use high walls to allow the ground floor to open up to the outside and the south-facing garden.

Architect Driss Kettani left the street facade of the north-south plot largely blank and mysterious, with vertical slats covering the street-facing windows. The house is accessed along a raised walkway of steps leading straight into a generous open-plan living area, two sides of which are glazed and overlook the garden. A run of curtains acts as a diaphanous barrier to the outside world, while the white floors, walls, and ceilings are juxtaposed with the central fireplace unit, which has a dark wood finish, and a slender wooden screen set at 90 degrees. There is also a tiled wall that runs from outside the entrance to the interior hall. Three bedrooms and a master suite with an adjoining terrace are located on the first floor, and there is a basement space below.

Villa Agava makes use of several traditional elements where appropriate, such as the tiles in the swimming pool, but the overall effect is white-walled modernism, although of course this reflects the long tradition of unadorned, simple domestic architecture in the region. The traditional courtyard is also referenced by the carefully separated planting zones, which create a set of outdoor rooms around the house. This outside space was landscaped by Atelier Bertrand Houin and divided into three sequences: a "mineral garden" at the entrance, an aquatic sequence at the side and a "vegetal garden" at the south end of the site. Kettani describes the project as a "play on the notions of privacy and transparency, fluidity and functional considerations." From the street, it gives little away; inside, Villa Agava conjures up a hidden contemporary world that still has a strong link to the world outside.

1 An all-white interior mirrors the pristine quality of the exterior walls. 2 A gated townhouse, Villa Agava presents an air of mystery to the street. Overleaf Bespoke timber screens divide the living space.

MILELE HOUSE

A traditional Swahili-style dwelling, renovated and enhanced by Urko Sanchez Architects, Milele House is located on the coast of Lamu Island, about 250 miles (400 km) northeast of Mombasa. The original architectural style evolved from a melange of Islamic and Arabic influences, all filtered through the traditional building methods and materials of East Africa. The house is centered around two courtyards—described by the architects as "serene spaces from which all other rooms emerge"—which are a typical feature of the architecture of the region. Accommodation is arranged over three stories, with a roof terrace that enjoys views over the Indian Ocean. Lamu itself is a UNESCO World Heritage Site, and this restoration project has ensured that the key original elements are still in place, such as the Makuti thatch roof construction, made from densely woven palm leaves.

The two courtyards allow for natural cross ventilation, the first with a staircase leading to the upper floors and the second with a small pool. Additional natural cooling is provided by the planting, with palm trees on the rear patio to shade the pool and bougainvillea plants on the upper terraces to help keep the strong sun away from the verandas. The main living and dining spaces are located on the ground floor, with the bedrooms on the upper two floors, looking inward to the main patio courtyard. An external stair leads to the roof terrace.

The entire structure of Milele House was restored and built using manual labor. Lamu Island is a car-free zone and all materials therefore had to be transported by donkey. Wherever possible, local materials were used, including coral stone, lime plaster, the Makuti thatch, and square lintels of iroko wood, or mvule, carved by local artisans. The wall of niches for display and storage is a common element in Swahili-style architecture. Overall, the effect is strikingly modern yet still directly connected to an architecture with many centuries of history behind it.

| 1 | 2 |

1 One of the internal courtyards at Milele House contains a small pool.   2 The main courtyard features a traditional galleried staircase.

CAPE TOWN

As the heart of South Africa's government and a major port with many centuries of history, Cape Town has always been one of the most cosmopolitan parts of a country that has a torturous history of colonialism, inequality, and naked segregation. Apartheid's immediate legacy was the segregation of what had been, by South African standards, a relatively diverse city. The centrally located District 6 was effectively emptied, demolished, and reassigned to whites-only residents in the 1970s and 1980s, with racist ideology destroying decades of organic urban growth. Understandably, the modern city is highly sensitive to its history, perhaps more so than most, with the close proximity of the apartheid-era prison on Robben Island and the region's long-standing role as South Africa's prime tourist destination.

Before politics intervened, Cape Town was shaped by geography. Set in a natural bowl, with the sawn-off peak of Table Mountain dominating the skyline, the city expanded around the edges of Table Bay to the north and False Bay to the south. The central business district lies just south of the docks, while suburbs of varying degrees of prosperity are strung out from the city, wrapped around the slopes of the rocky outcrops that dominate downtown views. As would be expected from its long and complex colonial heritage, Cape Town is rich with historic architecture, in particular the synthesis form known as Cape Dutch. This blend of influences from traditional northern European residential architecture, particularly from France, Germany, and the Netherlands, and Indonesian style brought a familiar domesticity to the region, with white-walled, low-built structures, often with prominent central gables, dormer windows, and shutters.

Like all dominant modes of vernacular architecture, Cape Dutch has survived to the present day, although strictly accurate reinterpretations are rare. For the most part, the gabled style is recreated in pastiche and overt symbolism, dovetailing with modernism's traditional reliance on the white wall plane as a symbol of progress, simplicity, and modernity. A cursory study of the residential architecture built in and around the city in the past two decades shows a huge disparity between the sleek but generic suburban villas and the invariably "undesigned" dwellings erected in the townships—the dense, unregulated urban areas that grew directly out of apartheid-era policies.

There are concerted efforts to improve township living conditions through design. Urban-Think Tank's Empower Shack uses a modular system that attempts to codify and sanction the *ad hoc* nature of township building, improving living spaces, sanitation, and security. The design itself can be scaled to fit with the site and economic conditions, thus allowing growth and change of use to be

accommodated without compromising the integrity of the building. Other innovative initiatives include the POD-Idladla, a small-scale prefabricated house that can be grouped together to make larger dwellings. Designed by Clara da Cruz Almeida and made in South Africa, the POD is a reaction against the relentless upsizing of the region's standalone private houses.

Projects such as these small-scale experiments stand in stark contrast to the traditional take on modernism that continues to dominate the local architectural press, parlaying the seductive visuals of modern design against the backdrop of the Cape climate. Yet there is also a move toward improving the suburbs, revisiting traditional housing types such as terraces with a sympathetic but dynamic modern approach. Although Cape Town's situation is atypical, it shares its suburban and urban conditions with many other centuries-old towns around the world, with a surfeit of out-of-date housing stock that nevertheless forms a well-functioning and human-scale streetscape. Renovation or revival is often a much better course of action than wholesale reconstruction.

In recent years, the city's image has been transformed by the opening of the Zeitz Museum of Contemporary Art Africa

1 The Zeitz Museum of Contemporary Art Africa is located on the city's V&A Waterfront. Designed by Heatherwick Studio, it opened in 2017.   2 A view of downtown Cape Town, with Table Mountain in the distance.

3

4

Heatherwick Studio's grandiose re-purposing of a former grain silo on the V&A Waterfront. In collaboration with local studios Van der Merwe Miszewski Architects, Jacobs Parker Architects, and Rick Brown and Associates, Heatherwick worked with the original concrete to create a virtuoso interior atrium around a gallery dedicated to the world's largest collection of contemporary African art, with a new boutique hotel on the upper floors. The V&A Waterfront was already the most visited tourist destination in Cape Town. Like many modern cities, Cape Town is following the playbook of cultural improvement as a means of social engagement. In addition to the undeniable social and cultural importance of sites such as Robben Island and District 6, Cape Town is arguably adopting the Bilbao model, with signature architecture acting as a catalyst for regeneration, attracting visitors and buoying up the local economy. Yet, with so much of the city's sprawling suburbs—with a total population of around 3.7 million—still struggling against the setbacks generated by such a repressive century, the power of design can only play second fiddle to politics.

1 A simple modular system uses everyday building materials. 2 The building type can be replicated in terraces at different scales.

EMPOWER SHACK

The Empower Shack is the result of a cross-continental collaboration between the Urban-Think Tank at the Swiss Institute of Technology (ETH) in Zurich and development partners in Cape Town, including Ikhayalami and the community of Khayelitsha in the BT Section (Site C). The project sought to develop a housing model that would supersede the sub-standard residences found in many of South Africa's dense urban townships. Growth there is unchecked and unregulated, which leads to issues of space, privacy, sanitation, and development.

The Empower Shack uses readily available local building materials, including breeze blocks, wood, and corrugated metal, to create a terraced form that can be infinitely adjusted and customized by residents for living and working. The two-story housing prototype is only one of three essential components for change and improvement, the others being the need for a new approach to spatial planning and

livelihood. Architecture is integral, yet aesthetics are subsumed by more urgent needs. The developers and collaborators from ETH created a new interface between the community, local professionals and the government, thereby allowing for self-determined development and for funds and resources to be diverted efficiently. South Africa's modern urban landscape has been shaped by the Reconstruction and Development Program (RDP), instigated by Nelson Mandela's ANC in 1994, to address the socio-economic divides created by apartheid.

Economics are a fundamental component of the design, with micro-financing available as well as an income-generating renewable energy model. The design is highly flexible, capable of providing six different units configured into a row-house typology. The unit is formed from a mixture of prefabricated components and off-the-shelf building materials. High ceilings and open circulation aid natural

3 Building materials and processes are designed to use available local skills. 4 Each "shack" is offered as a shell. 5 Construction is quick and straightforward. 6 Interior specifications can be pared back to suit the budget.

ventilation and, depending on user affordability, the units can be upgraded to include additional internal partitions, external balconies, fitted kitchens, and interior finishes. Custom digital tools make planning more straightforward, ensuring that residents' choices can be synthesized into the positioning of the new buildings, thus preserving social and commercial groupings without compromising existing relationships.

Low-budget housing is a significant design challenge in many parts of the world. Improving existing housing stock is often frustrated by planning and infrastructure conditions. The Empower Shack presents a holistic view of housing, exploring and utilizing the accumulated knowledge, capacity, and organization of local residents to support the direct improvement of their living environment.

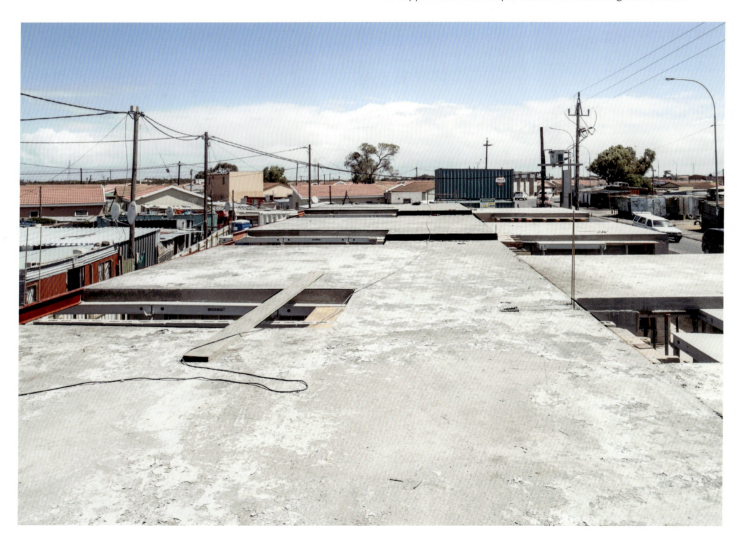

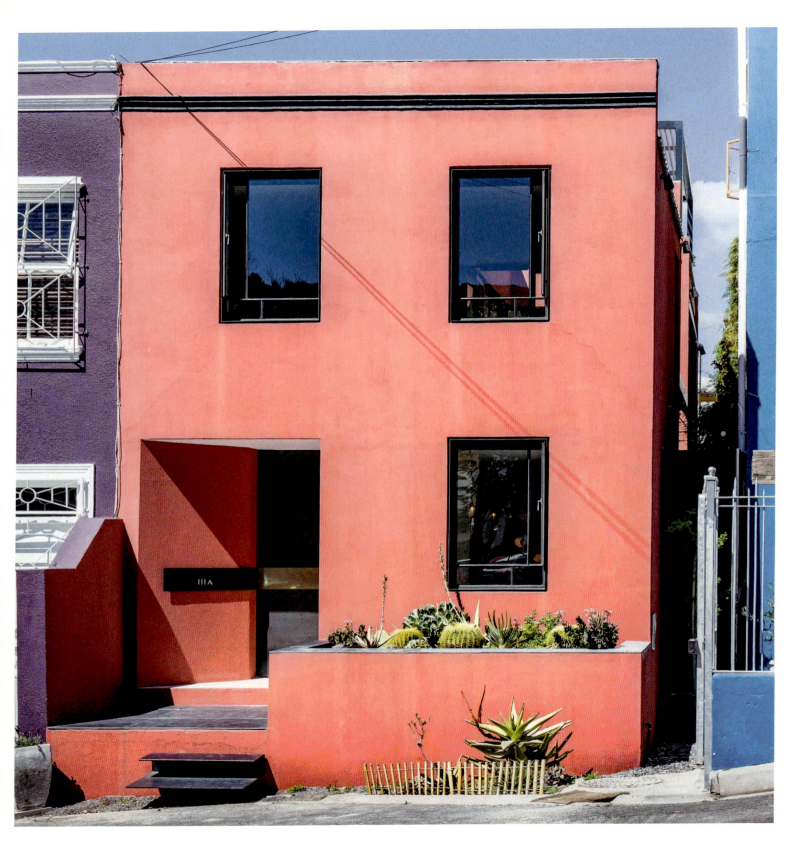

1   A traditionally colorful Bo-Kaap exterior is subtly
enhanced by new additions.   2 Simple modern interior
finishes contrast with the bright exterior.

HOUSE IIIA

Located in the heart of one of Cape Town's most historic areas, a Grade I National Conservation Area, House IIIA is an investigation into how contemporary design can be brought into a traditional context, using the language of the original vernacular but radically revising the planning, materials, and details. House IIIA is a row house, albeit one that was built relatively recently. At only twenty-five years old, the terrace was constructed to be sympathetic to the scale and massing of the more traditional housing in the Bo-Kaap area of Cape Town. In radically refurbishing the structure, The Fold Architects decided to retain the fundamental proportions of the facade while conducting comprehensive interior restructuring to make the house more suited to modern life.

The two-story House IIIA contains kitchen, dining, and living spaces at the entrance level, with two bedrooms above. Although the rooms remain conventionally sized, the architects expanded the living area by incorporating a new staircase into the open-plan design. Another addition is the roof garden, which gives spectacular views across the city toward Table Mountain. A shaded seating area and fish pond are joined by a large roof light above the new staircase. The last is fabricated from mild steel and assembled as a series of "S"-fold stair treads, each cantilevered from the wall and also top hung by a series of fasteners that double up as slender metal balustrades.

The first-floor landing also includes metal elements, with a floor panel made from metal slats in homage to the light industrial heritage of the area. These allow more light to reach the sunken lounge below. A further exterior space is provided on the first floor, set in between the two bedrooms. A private external courtyard, open to the sky and the exterior wall, it was placed to generate interesting vistas through, across, and out of the house. The striking red color

3 A roof terrace offers far-reaching views to Table Mountain.   4 The folded steel staircase is top hung to maximize space.

3

4

used for all the rendered walls adds a final layer of visual interest in an area characterized by solid, bold hues. Inside, in addition to the use of metal, the primary materials are concrete and light and dark woods. The former is left exposed in the kitchen counter and pillars, combined with custom black door and window frames, patterned tiles, dark floors, and bronze detailing in lights, switches, and taps to create an unexpectedly rich and varied interior. The narrow alley to the side of the house has been re-purposed as a two-story vertical garden, visible through the glazed walls in the living and dining areas, bedroom two and the upstairs courtyard. The interior of the house, therefore, becomes a retreat from the city, without compromising the important contribution the facade makes to the neighborhood.

The street facade presents itself as a solid block of color, with unconventional details such as the metal steps hinting at what is inside. A recessed entrance door and deep window reveals add shadows and relief to the facade, evoking the traditional structure of these archetypal row houses.

1 The Burj Khalifa not only heralded a new era for design and architecture in the United Arab Emirates and wider region, but it also remains the tallest building in the world to date.

ASIA

BEIJING SEOUL GANGNEUNG-SI
GYEONGGI-DO TOKYO AHMEDABAD
JAMMU COLOMBO BANGKOK
HO CHI MINH CITY KUALA LUMPUR
SINGAPORE JAKARTA

2 The Beijing Olympics helped China to show off its sporting, cultural and architectural clout, while the skyscrapers in the capital's Central Business District, seen here behind the Worker's Stadium, rose to signify the country's economic might.

Trying to reduce a continent as big and as complex as Asia down to a single architectural approach seems futile; however, there are a number of common threads and trends within its many diverse countries that help to weave a multivoiced yet coherent narrative for this particularly dynamic part of the world. With the continent's major powerhouses—China, Japan, and India—having already established themselves as key international players in the financial and cultural fields by the noughties, other contenders are now beginning to emerge, battling to take over the top spots in Asia's thriving and ever-changing architectural scene. Countries such as South Korea and Singapore have made rapid advances in recent years, leading the way globally in design and technology, with a business-minded and culture-savvy market. Furthermore, Vietnam, Indonesia, Malaysia, and the Philippines are also experiencing exponential growth, resulting in a real construction and architectural boom in the region. This is assisted by the fact that these are some of the most populous nations in the continent, with some of the youngest populations.

Not so long ago, at the turn of the century, it felt as if China was an unstoppable force. The Beijing Olympics (2008), with all its associated wonders, was just around the corner, characterizing a decade in which the country firmly staked its place on the world architecture map. China proudly flaunted its wealth and power through world-class events, transforming into the cultural and industrial force that it is today and establishing itself as an important manufacturing hub and a center for Asian art and design. In the meantime, India's modernist legacy was still reigning supreme. Alongside it, a number of the country's emerging architects began to explore their contemporary identity, drawing from their rich history and craft heritage. Between these two countries, Asia accounted for two of the four up-and-coming

3 In Mumbai, new luxury high-rise residential blocks can be found side by side with India's infamous slums.

BRIC nations (Brazil, Russia, India, and China)—the world's leading, fast-emerging, developing economies at the time.

Across the sea, Japan's understated, historically inspired, and craft-rich minimalism was a constant global source of inspiration, as was the country's more experimental, technology-informed, and futuristic approach. Architects such as Toyo Ito, Kenzo Tange, Kengo Kuma, and Tadao Ando have been not only critical in defining their country's architectural scene during the second half of the twentieth century and the twenty-first century, but are also internationally acknowledged for their respective contributions to shaping global architecture history. Further west, Dubai was flying the flag for the Middle East, with the United Arab Emirates blazing the trail for design in the region and showcasing it with the world's tallest building, the Burj Khalifa. Completed in 2008, the skyscraper has more than 160 stories, is the world's tallest free-standing structure and has the highest observation deck in the world. At the turn of the century, it seemed that Asia was about to reach its peak; now, a new wave of power and creativity coming out of the continent is about to prove this wrong.

Identified by some experts to be among the world's fastest-emerging markets today, the next BRICs include Bangladesh, Indonesia, Pakistan, the Philippines, South Korea, and Vietnam, as well as—lest we forget, Asia is not just the Far East—Iran and Turkey. Furthermore, Abu Dhabi's Saadiyat Island already rivals Dubai's architectural marvels and world-class tourism, featuring a cultural district that is set to include attractions such as a Louvre museum by Jean Nouvel, a Guggenheim by Frank Gehry, the Zayed National Museum by Foster + Partners and the Abu Dhabi Performing Arts Centre by Zaha Hadid. While the Western design world appears to be in a transition period—in which the older league of starchitects are nearing retirement age and the younger generation are seeking to define their own style while coming out of a global financial crisis—the world's eyes have turned to Asia, which houses not only some of the most promising economies, but also some of the most populous countries and most exciting creative industries. These countries have the knack to design, and also the skill and manpower to produce, which is proving to be a winning combination.

The 2010s is a good time to be an architect in Asia. Money is becoming more readily available, with local wealthy patrons and enterprising developers investing in the region. At the same time, the aspiring, rising middle classes are seeking to make the most of their growing assets and are willing to experiment, showing off their refined, educated, and design-led tastes. Growth never comes without challenges, though, and housing is among the region's key issues, as each nation is attempting to tackle its increasing population and, in numerous instances, social inequalities. Large mass-housing residential blocks make up whole chunks of the urban fabric, contrasted, in many cases, by low-rise and poor-quality tenements, often sitting side by side with luxurious villas in a true melange of socioeconomic strata.

Adding to this rapid urbanization—a phenomenon encountered in numerous Asian cities, and in most capitals—many parts of the continent have been left trying to grapple with a dense and hastily built environment. This has led to several urbanistic challenges that further blight the residents' quality of life and prospects, such as traffic circulation and air pollution. Combining these rapid advances with the preservation of architectural and wider cultural heritage is starting to appear high on the agenda of many of these countries, who are attempting to find ways to establish a meaningful balance between past, present, and future. Areas of historical compounds, such as Beijing's hutong clusters and Seoul's hanok houses, are examples of architecture that is topping these lists.

At the same time, following years of Western influence, many Asian architects have embarked on an exploration of their own regional identities, as a way to reconcile the new and the old in a search that is seen by many as an important and necessary step towards the continent's real autonomy and prosperity. What is Asian design, and what is its context? What does it mean to be a creative in this part of the world today? When each area's native crafts, materials, construction techniques, climatic restrictions, and traditions are combined with the architecture professionals' world-class knowledge and skill, talents abound throughout the continent, and the answers to these questions—and more—are finally within reach.

BEIJING

There is no better representation of modern-day China and the country's drive, dynamism, and aspiration than its capital, Beijing. It is one of the Four Great Ancient Capitals of China and the home of no fewer than seven UNESCO World Heritage Sites. It was also the heart of the Cultural Revolution and where Mao Zedong declared the formation of the People's Republic of China, slowly transforming the country into the powerhouse it is today. Beijing is a city that has thrived and prospered, made it through wars and turbulences, and lived to tell the tale—and it has the architecture to prove it.

The city's intense urbanization over the past few decades has transformed parts of it beyond recognition. Evidence of Beijing's imperial past is not so apparent any more, even though important landmarks, such as the Forbidden City and Tiananmen Square, remain. The housing stock reflects this. Historical houses are few and far between, considering the city's size, and they include traditional hutongs: low clusters of modest housing, arranged tightly together through a system of alleyways. This type of courtyard residence was prevalent during the Qing and Ming dynasties, but began to disappear in the late twentieth century to make way for modern buildings and infrastructure. Their prominent position in the heart of the capital meant that they were sitting on prime land for redevelopment, to be taken over for new roads, housing, and commercial buildings. With Beijing's rapid urbanization in the early noughties gathering pace, and hutongs swiftly being razed to the ground, a debate developed in the city's architecture circles arguing for the preservation of the few remaining clusters. Now, with demolition slowing down, the capital's culture-savvy middle classes have been campaigning to save what is left of this aspect of Beijing's architectural legacy.

The Chinese capital's historic fabric sits side by side with communist period mega-blocks—some for office use and many for housing. This Sino-Soviet style (Chinese architects and urban planners of the time drew heavily on their Soviet peers for inspiration in both theory and looks) can be found in several "key" cities across China, as part of the country's centralized plans for economic and industrial development. The tower blocks produced as a result were mostly created in the 1950s, 1960s, and 1970s, and still form part of Beijing's suburbs.

The turn of the century and the announcement of Beijing as the host of the 2008 Olympic Games changed everything. The city entered an era of intense construction, creating one iconic structure after another, eager to show off its flair and power to the world. Starchitects from all around the globe flocked to the Chinese capital to work their magic. The Bird's Nest stadium by Herzog & de Meuron and Ai Weiwei, the CCTV headquarters by OMA, the

National Aquatics Centre by Chris Bosse and Rob Leslie-Carter of PTW Architects, and the ultramodern new international airport by Foster + Partners were all created at the start of the millennium, and are some of the several landmark buildings that helped Beijing firmly mark its place in the contemporary global architecture scene.

Housing soon followed, and the city grew and grew, almost doubling in size in the first decade of the twenty-first century. Private developers joined the government in the construction boom. The Linked Hybrid by Steven Holl is a fitting representative of a modern Beijing housing block, created by a local private developer, Modern Green Development Co. It combines a mostly residential element with open-air spaces and some commercial units on the ground level. It also incorporates green strategies and a carefully articulated facade and volume design. The award-winning project was named Best Tall Building in 2009 by the Council on Tall Buildings and Urban Habitat.

The fast pace of Beijing's change and the prominent role of Western architects gave birth to a new debate: what does contemporary Chinese architecture look like? Local architects got stuck into their responses, and housing became a significant part of their portfolio. One recent example is Chaoyang Park Plaza by MAD

1 Steven Holl's Linked Hybrid is one of the several modern residential complexes created in Beijing by international architects in recent years.   2 Beijing's traditional housing stock used to include several clusters of hutongs, the Chinese capital's famous complexes of small courtyard houses; many have now been razed to the ground.

led by Ma Yansong. This luxury mixed-use development includes a strong residential element and seeks to redefine Chinese architecture through its eye-catching shapes. Such growth did not come without problems. Beijing's air pollution is notorious, as the city struggles to deal with the rapidly changing urban realm and circulation of the past few decades. Bicycles are still used in great numbers, but they can do little to help when up against a huge increase in population and built space. In fact, Beijing authorities have recently been discussing imposing a limit on the many bike-sharing schemes to avoid putting further vehicles on the already heavily congested roads.

Today, Beijing is a global megalopolis, featuring a mixture of housing, a sea of modern office blocks, a busy transport system and a selection of cultural offerings. New projects, such as the Guardian Art Centre by Ole Scheeren, demonstrate how the city's architectural renaissance surrounding the Olympics was not a one-off event, but an ongoing journey for this ambitious capital. Named a "City of Design" by UNESCO in 2012, Beijing is keen to show off its expanding creative network, which includes design, the arts, and, of course, architecture.

3 The Beijing National Stadium, affectionately known as the Bird's Nest, was designed by Swiss architecture practice Herzog & de Meuron, in collaboration with Ai Weiwei who acted as an artistic consultant.   4 Chaoyang Park Plaza is one of the latest mixed-use developments in Beijing created by MAD, the architecture practice headed by Ma Yansong and one of the country's leading home-grown firms.

BEIJING
COUNTRY China
ARCHITECT Arch Studio   YEAR 2015

1 Chinese architecture firm Arch Studio transformed a traditional hutong into a contemporary family home.   2 The architects kept a neutral color palette in order to create a crisp, clean interior atmosphere.

WHITE HOUSE

Beijing's frenzied construction boom during the twentieth century made the Chinese capital the global metropolis it is today, but it also led to the demolition of many of the city's traditional hutongs—the famous groupings of courtyard houses linked by narrow alleyways, which were first established in the city as early as the thirteenth century. Until recently, many hutongs were still thriving in the heart of Beijing. Most of these have now been razed to the ground to be replaced by large-scale concrete housing developments, new roads, and office buildings. However, more recently, a movement for the preservation of Beijing's few remaining hutongs has been gathering pace, headed by prominent architects, academics, and urban planners, and China's growing affluent middle class has begun to buy them, in order to save and update the dwellings for the twenty-first century.

Nestled in the hutong of Dongcheng District, White House, by locally based Arch Studio, is an example of a contemporary redesign of a traditional hutong dwelling. Constructed in gray brick and concrete, the house used to follow the representative hutong typology: a modest house squeezed together with five more similar structures. The old building had no outside space and felt dark and cramped, because opening up windows and looking out compromised the owners' privacy.

Arch Studio principal Han Wenqiang decided to tackle this issue by completely re-imagining the hutong from the inside out, while keeping its iconic external volume. Fully gutting the old structure, taking down walls and partitions, the architects opened up the interiors to create a "bright, transparent and clean atmosphere," while maintaining its external appearance so as not to affect the character of the old city block. By using the color white to cover everything, from walls to ceilings, floors, and dividing screens, Arch Studio injected a modern sense of minimalism into the house,

unifying the interior, while managing to bring natural light deep inside the floor plate. Bare brick on the exterior walls was maintained, but spray painted white, so as to bridge old and new.

In order to improve the internal flow, the architects cut a large opening through the floor slabs, inserting a crisp new staircase at the building's core. Crossing all levels, this opening also acts as a light shaft, bringing sunshine deep into the heart of the home. Made out of elegant ¾-inch (2 cm) steel, the clean geometric form of the stair features 2-inch (5 cm) perforated steel handrails, and serves as a piece of fine sculpture, as much as the house's main circulation core.

The home's spectacular built-in bookcase lines the walls of the living space and is a key visual feature in the internal arrangement, as well as functional bespoke storage. The shelves not only host the owners' increasing book collection, but also create a pleasing fine grid pattern against the simple white walls. A glass pavilion pushes through the structure's very top, leading up to an accessible terrace. Here, the owners are able to enjoy the sense of openness that the surrounding low roofs provide, and can look out over the neighboring trees and take in the area's urban beauty and the Beijing skyline beyond.

3 A central staircase with perforated steel handrails cuts through all levels.   4 Today, many Chinese architects return to the hutong typology, redesigning it for the twenty-first century.   5 A glass pavilion leads visitors up to a roof terrace.

1 | 2 | 3

MICRO-HUTONG

Beijing's housing followed traditional patterns of development for many centuries. The hutong is a form of urbanism particular to the city, comprising long narrow alleys that are formed from the close proximity of small courtyard residences, known as siheyuan. The siheyuan is a dense archetype, formed from four low (usually single-story) buildings arranged around a central courtyard. The arrangement of the living quarters, the decoration of the entrance way, and the alignment of the structures were all in accordance with elements of traditional Chinese philosophy and morality.

The rapid urbanization of Beijing has seen the loss of many thousands of these historic dwellings. Standarchitecture's Micro-Hutong project is an attempt to update the original model for the modern era, using the same restrictive area without compromising space, light, or privacy. At only 375 square feet (35 sq m), the Micro-Hutong is extremely modest. The primary street-fronting space is a small gallery with a traditional tiled pitched roof. Behind this is a U-shaped courtyard containing the living areas. The architects describe it as a "flexible urban living room," a space that serves as a transition between the public street and the private zones of the house. Two trees are also planted here to provide a minimal green outlook.

Finished in board-marked concrete, with large glazed apertures, the plan uses a complex set of angles to avoid overlooking between the different modules. These cantilevered modules house the bedroom, study room, teahouse, dining room, and bathroom. The cast concrete is mixed with Chinese ink, emphasizing the streaks between the layers of each pour. The house is designed to be naturally ventilated, with opening skylights allowing fresh air to circulate into the deep, cave-like plan. With the onset of Beijing's cold winters, the heated floors make the interior warm and inviting. Zhang Ke's studio, standarchitecture, has reinterpreted this traditional dwelling by accentuating the flexibility afforded by the courtyard arrangement. Although small in scale, it provides a grand architectural experience.

FAIRYLAND GUORUI VILLAS

Beijing's fast-paced development of the past few decades led to a lot of sizeable housing being erected pretty swiftly in the city's vast suburbs, yet not all larger-scale residential schemes fit the stereotype of the monolithic block. In fact, architecturally led, low-rise housing developments have started to make their appearance everywhere in the country, addressing the needs of the rising design-aware, well-traveled, and often internationally educated middle classes of China—and foreign architects have joined the game, including high-profile names such as David Chipperfield. The Fairyland Guorui Villa complex, in the Chinese capital's Miyun Economic & Technical Development Zone 1, follows a similar approach.

The development comprises fifty-six single-family houses set beautifully and generously among natural greenery and manicured landscaping, created by acclaimed Dutch-based practice UNStudio for the Guorui Group. The site, which is located right at the point where two rivers converge, offers a striking combination of both water and mountain views. In order to make the most of the beautiful setting, the architects incorporated into their master plan communal areas such as nature-led boulevards (there is one riverside and one tree-lined) and a shared garden for the owners. The aim was to create a vibrant community among the residents and a place that would allow them to commune seamlessly with nature.

While the complex has a unified approach and visual identity, each villa has a slightly different volume configuration. Created in sculptural, clay-colored, recycled-stone formations, the houses' facades vary with a mix of inside and outside spaces, such as windows, canopies, terraces, and roof gardens. These variations, featuring UNStudio's signature curves and modern shapes, were

1 This complex bears the signature swooping curves and flowing forms of its creator, UNStudio. 2 The structures are clad in thin stone units that follow the ambitious curves. 3 The sculptural houses reflect the organic shapes of the nearby river and flora.

carefully calculated to be distinctive enough to encourage diversity and uniqueness, but also standardized enough to be able to support efficient construction and visual consistency throughout the development. The undulating nature of the design, matched with the cladding's thin stone units, creates an almost pixelated effect that gives out a soft overall impression, reflecting the organic shapes of the surrounding rivers and flora. The houses' natural shapes and colors make them blend effortlessly into the site's greenery and waters, helping to underline the complex's smooth connection between the natural and the man-made.

Inside, the villas follow an open-plan arrangement, as dictated by UNStudio's design intention. However, different interiors firms handled individual designs. Consequently, the houses come in a variety of layouts and include several rooms, ensuring there are suitable spaces for interaction among inhabitants, privacy, and rest.

The development was designed to be sustainability conscious, which was a key concern for the team, given the capital's past environmental woes and the site's delicate eco system. The architects used passive techniques to control heat gain and loss. Advanced heat insulation contributes to the same, while the structures' energy needs are at least partially covered by the use of solar and wind power. Taking into account Beijing's air-quality challenges, the team incorporated a state-of-the-art ventilation system in the complex. This removes nearly all of the unwanted and unhealthy particles and provides clean and healthy air for the residents.

4 Each house is slightly different in order to encourage diversity and uniqueness.   5 The clay-colored external skin helps to create smooth transitions between the natural and the man-made.

SEOUL

Perfectly preserved historical palaces, some of the world's leading electronics brands, a largely traditional family-orientated society, and K-pop all exist side by side in Seoul, one of Asia's hottest destinations. The South Korean capital is multifaceted and thriving—having recently ranked highly in reviews for livability and sustainability—while its fast-growing market places it among the largest urban economies around. This is a global megacity that knows how to raise the bar. Named World Design Capital and UNESCO City of Design in 2010, and home to a range of iconic new buildings (such as Zaha Hadid's Dongdaemun Design Plaza), Seoul is on a mission to flaunt its architectural flair, too, which it has in spades.

You would expect nothing less than excellence in all fields from the world's "most wired city," and Seoul strives to make sure it remains on the cutting edge in the architecture department. In fact, design has been part of the city's official agenda since its first city architect, Seung H-Sang, was formally announced back in 2014. Created by the then-mayor, Park Won-soon, this role has been crucial in Seoul's exploration of its architectural identity—an ongoing

project. Now, the position has been taken over by Seung's successor, Kim Young-joon, who shares his drive and ambition to make this city a more architecturally aware and prominent one. Furthermore, given that approximately 73 percent of South Korea's designers are concentrated in Seoul, according to the Cities of Design Network, there is plenty of talent to work with.

A range of city initiatives explore different areas of the topic in question. There is a dedicated team working with the city architect to not only oversee various aspects in the process of realizing public works, but also to raise awareness for design. Seoul's inaugural Biennale of Architecture and Urbanism, launched in October 2017, helps toward the latter, while fittingly investigating the development, growth, and future of modern cities as part of its program. An element of the former is the city's latest flagship in urbanism and landscape design, Seoullo 7017. Also known as the Skygarden, this is Seoul's version of the High Line in New York City: a disused elevated 1970s highway that has been transformed into a pedestrian bridge, full of plants and resting spots, by Dutch architecture firm MVRDV.

It forms both an essential part of the city's circulation system and a pleasant promenade for locals and tourists.

On the residential front, Seoul is a real mix of scales and styles. Spread across a hilly terrain, the city features several mountains, which create a beautiful and diverse urban scenery and define different neighborhoods. Some are made up of modern high rises and some are lower residential ones, featuring an eclectic mix of new and older properties. The traditional Korean hanok houses are now rare, but they can still be found in places. In many cases, though, preserved historical clusters have been redesigned for leisure and retail, as seen at the Bukchon Hanok Village. As with many an Asian capital, Seoul experienced rapid urbanization throughout the second half of the twentieth century, steadily rising to its 10-million-strong population today. This resulted in parts of the city being fairly rapidly and densely built, thereby creating challenges for residents and architects alike. At the same time, the fact that whole areas were completely destroyed during World War II means that, although this city has been around for centuries, it still feels—at least in places—entirely new.

This situation gave local architects ample ground for experimentation, and they have been making the most of it. Seoul has a rich variety of modern housing, some thoroughly contemporary, influenced by current international trends and created in sweeping curves, unconventional layouts, and bold material combinations; others are inspired by historical Korean architecture, featuring traditional courtyards and pitched roofs. However, in a country where the old sits hand in hand with the new, no matter how much a home is inspired by historical typologies, avant-garde technologies can still play a key role. In this tech-savvy nation, most new homes have clever digital systems that control services at the push of a button, usually simply monitored from the resident's mobile phone.

At the same time, Seoul's growing population and increasing need for housing have put pressure on the city's architects to create ever more space- and cost-efficient buildings in order to satisfy market demand and regulatory constraints. Often focusing on the ratio of a building's total floor area to the size of the plot, these limitations form a common theme in many new projects and represent one of the biggest challenges Seoul's—and the wider country's—architects face. So prevalent is the issue that it became the theme examined in the Korean Pavilion at the Venice Architecture Biennale in 2016.

Still, despite demanding site restrictions and complicated planning regulations, practices such as System Lab, OBBA, and JOHO Architecture have turned their hand to both single-family private houses and boutique apartment blocks, which dot the South Korean capital in innovative, daring designs. Among them is a thriving residential typology: the multigenerational home. In this family-orientated culture, it is not uncommon for several generations to live under one roof, with extended families sharing a single design. Local

1 Traditional hanok houses once defined Seoul's housing stock; now only a few small clusters remain, having given way to redevelopment.   2 Lotte World Tower was designed by Kohn Pedersen Fox and completed in 2016. It not only makes for an instantly recognizable landmark in Seoul, but is also the fifth-tallest building in the world to date.

3 Rapid growth and architectural ambition mean that Seoul is a true mix of old and new, with low-rise housing neighborhoods sitting next to state-of-the-art skyscrapers and brand new districts.   **4** This private gallery and house, located in the hills of the Kangbuk section of Seoul, was created by US architect Steven Holl.

architects' responses to this particular brief are varied and have led to some of the city's most ingenious homes. Furthermore, while Seoul firms seem to be behind the vast majority of the city's handsome residential stock, international practices have also joined in, with names such as New York-based Steven Holl and Belgian architect Julien De Smedt working on projects in town, designing the Daeyang Gallery and House, and a large-scale housing block in the popular district of Gangnam, respectively.

Drawing from its rich past but firmly looking toward the future, Seoul has plenty to offer to residential architecture. In a place where starchitects and large global firms produce eye-catching retail and cultural spaces and sleek glass towers (KPF's Lotte World Tower, which includes housing, is the fifth-tallest building in the world to date), local architects remain prolific in their contribution to the advancement of the humble Korean home. And with an enterprising, business-minded and highly design-aware government and clientele, this is clearly just the beginning for Seoul; watch this space.

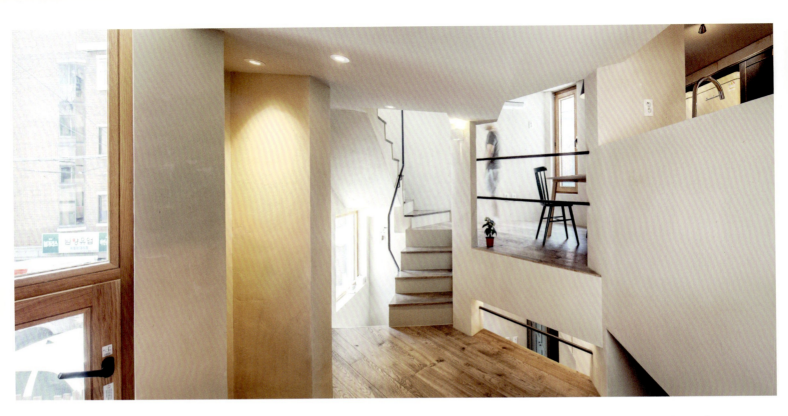

SEOUL

COUNTRY South Korea
ARCHITECT ThePlus Architects **YEAR** 2017

1 Tightly wedged into its plot, the house's many floors are united by a winding staircase. 2 Crevice House stands in pristine contrast to its *ad hoc* surroundings.

CREVICE HOUSE

ThePlus Architects' Crevice House occupies "a small piece of land in a big city." As its name suggests, it physically resembles a sliver of light, standing in stark contrast to its surroundings. The irregular plot is only 605 square feet (56 sq m), and the new house appears to have been carved and chamfered to fit precisely within it. From the basement workshop up to the tower and roof terrace, this is a vertical space for a small family unit. Unwilling to leave the South Korean capital due to work and lifestyle, the clients eschewed the conventional in favor of a multilevel space that makes the most of the opportunities presented by the site.

The name "Crevice" ultimately drove every facet of the design. Twelve concrete floor slabs are united by a winding staircase, with each of the six floor levels split in two and offering a different function. This creates a series of views up and down and across the space, ensuring that the compact feeling of the house does

not become too oppressive. The architect has also used a range of window shapes, internal lighting, and a variety of materials to make this house as much about vertical connections as possible. The staircase rises up at the corner of the site, forming a protective screen for the more intimate spaces it encloses. Sunlight floods through the window at the southern corner, and windows are placed and angled to avoid overlooking the neighbors, thereby leading to some deep angular recesses that evoke castellated structures or rock formations. "Nearly every movement between spaces requires you to use the staircase," the architects note.

Crevice House faced the many difficulties of building on a restricted site and used them to its advantage. The basement workroom sits below a sitting room on the entrance level. Above this is the family kitchen and dining area, with two bedrooms on the floor above. The child's room is a double-height loft with mezzanine, while

the master suite is set across the upper three floors, with storage, wardrobes, and a powder room on the fourth floor and a spectacular bathroom in the eaves of the tower space on the roof.

Slotting a house between existing buildings presents numerous practical challenges. Here, the entrance alleyway was very narrow, which made unloading materials difficult, and the proximity of the site to the neighbors also prompted numerous complaints. However, the result—Crevice House—is a self-contained insular space, and also a distinctive and playful structure that enhances the urban realm.

3 Each floor is arranged over multiple levels, with views above and below.   4 Timber floors unify the space, with many views onto the external streets.   5 The basement utility area is given a different material treatment.

MOEBIUS HOUSE

The resort city of Gangneung-si on the east coast of South Korea is a popular tourist spot, renowned for its sunsets. Perched on one of the rolling hills, on a vantage point offering panoramic views of the city and seaside, Moebius House is the brainchild of Seoul-based architecture practice JOHO and its principal, Jeong Hoon Lee.

Occupying a narrow and oddly shaped plot of several irregular corners at the end of a sleepy residential cul-de-sac, the project follows the lines of its topography, keeping in dialogue with its context in more ways than one. The building's stone-clad overall form twists and turns to gently reflect the orientation and linearity of the street; it expands into the site to form a Moebius strip shape that transforms into the house's architectural volume. This in turn mirrors traces of the surrounding city, responding once more to its context.

Making the most of the views, the architect cleverly raised the house on pillars and placed the common areas at the top. So, the second floor hosts the living room, kitchen, and dining space. A long timber-decked terrace wraps around them, providing an al fresco alternative for socializing. The master bedroom sits right underneath, on the first floor, protected from views from neighboring buildings by an opaque wall. The exterior's tactile stone is contrasted by a sleek interior of wood and concrete.

In order to create a building that is sustainable and operates harmoniously with its location's temperate climate, Lee took extra care to plan spaces that are naturally shaded and can be protected from the region's strong sun. At the same time, strategically placed windows ensure heat is absorbed during the winter. High thermal insulation and a thoughtful ventilation system are also in place. This house is not just smart and modern in terms of its looks. Intelligent digital systems have been incorporated into the design, which means that facilities such as electricity, lighting, heating, and ventilation, as well as Wi-Fi, can be controlled at the push of a button.

1 JOHO orientated this stone-clad house toward the views.
2 Its unusual shape was designed to follow that of a Moebius strip.   3 The living areas take over the second floor.   4 A timber-decked terrace wraps around the main living spaces.

BOJEONG-DONG HOUSE

Multigenerational living is not a new concept in South Korea. Having several generations and family members living under one roof was, in fact, the most acceptable traditional structure up until the last decade, when family units started to become smaller, focusing more on the nuclear core of a couple and their children alone. Now, however, the tide has started to turn again, and socioeconomic changes mean that the idea of the extended family is returning. In order to counteract the country's rising property and living costs, especially in the large urban hubs, nuclear units are joining forces. This is exemplified by Bojeong-dong House, which was created for three sisters and their respective families.

Designed by the emerging Seongnam-si based architecture practice The_System Lab, the highly sculptural house is located in Gyeonggi-do, an area that makes up the suburbs and countryside surrounding the country's capital of Seoul. The structure's generous size is down to the fact that it needed to house three households—and three generations—under a single roof.

The clients' brief was specific, in that the purpose of the building was to help weave together the three sisters' families organically during daily life, but also to provide plenty of privacy when needed, thus respecting each resident's individuality. In order to achieve this, the structure was divided into one larger and two smaller residential units, all set within a dramatic volume of sweeping curves and turrets, arranged in a loosely L-shaped floor plan.

Spanning three floors and constructed using rough board-form concrete, Bojeong-dong House's striking expressive form is designed in a fairly traditional Korean style, following the country's historical typology of a courtyard house. A large open space in the heart of the main house acts as a central core, where all the residents can gather and socialize, at the same time merging inside and outside. Here, warm wooden floors offset the outer shell's rougher concrete nature. Stepping outside, the outdoor parts of the house consist of a leafy garden and an extensive wood-lined deck area. The smaller units also have access to several outdoors areas upstairs,

in the shape of good-sized terraces and balconies; each apartment also has its own independent living space on each floor.

The facades are dotted with openings, in order to bring plenty of natural light in and to maintain a close connection with the outside world. However, these were designed deliberately to be relatively small, "so that families don't feel exposed," explains the architect. They also create a playful sense of mystery as to what the building's function may be. In contrast, the openings toward the courtyard are much larger, providing visual contact with the outdoors and across different spaces within the house. At the same time, smooth curves, softened edges, and skylights ensure that the interior of Bojeong-dong House is softly lit and feels cocooning, warm, and welcoming, in line with its domestic use.

3 The structure cleverly conceals three different households under one roof.   4 Balconies, terraces, and a garden ensure all units within this multigenerational home enjoy some outside space.

TOKYO

Home to perhaps the most unique set of urban housing characteristics in the developed world, Tokyo continues to astound and impress with its rich variety of domestic architecture. Today, the city can lay claim to some of the highest real-estate prices in the world, and also some of the most carefully defined land-use patterns of any megacity. To those unfamiliar with Tokyo, a visit can be disorientating; the center is dense and layered, with elevated roads and railways threading through a mostly medium-rise cityscape, with malls and hotels often starting many stories above ground level and the signage and advertising seemingly far more intense (although perceptions are undoubtedly skewed and distorted by the Tokyo of modern cinema). This visual modernity is juxtaposed with long-surviving small street patterns and densely planted urban parks.

In among this cauldron of technology and tradition is a remarkably stable domestic property market, with individual private houses scattered cheek by jowl through the city's many suburban neighborhoods. Japanese vernacular design was often hailed as one of the precursors of early modernism, deemed inspirational for its

simplicity of form, absence of decoration, and pared-back approach to domestic interiors. In hindsight, the fascination for Western architects was less with culture than with aesthetics; the use of wooden framing, the strict grid of the tatami flooring and shoji screens appealed to the reductivist tendency of the new moderns, men (for the most part) who considered ornament as somehow offensive, bourgeois, and irrelevant.

There was also a frailty to this traditional vernacular. The Great Kanto earthquake of 1923 laid waste to much of Tokyo, destroying so many houses and other buildings that serious consideration was given to moving the capital elsewhere. World War II saw yet more destruction, but by then Tokyo had a thriving population of 3.5 million and intensive rebuilding was the only option. Postwar reconstruction was driven by the increasing emphasis on the importance of the family house, and the government used the private house as a means of stimulating the economy—not necessarily the physical house itself as a long-term investment, but the compact family unit and the building plot as a resource that could be reused again and again as needs, tastes, technologies, and designs changed. This partly explains the dizzying variety of domestic design that has come out of Japan in the modern era and, perhaps most significantly of all, the role that actual living plays in this variety.

It was a time of experimentation and expediency. Concrete was heralded as the material most resistant to both fire and earthquakes, and Japanese concrete technology became the world's most advanced, with no cultural hang-ups about using beautifully finished concrete as the primary surface both inside and outside a house. Prefabrication in the true factory-built sense of the word also became a major part of modern Japanese house-building culture, with big companies such as Toyota and Panasonic, and even retail brands like Muji, producing successful designs for off-the-shelf houses. The need for rapid reconstruction in the wake of natural disasters also led to innovation. The earthquakes of 1995 and 2011 saw many architect-driven solutions for small-scale temporary housing, most notably the cardboard tube structures pioneered by Shigeru Ban in Kobe in 1995.

Despite this culture of change and innovation, many Japanese have little time for the house as a pure aesthetic statement. Instead, the house forms a statement about lifestyle and the way in which one chooses to live one's life, rather than having tastes and desires filtered through the aesthetic sensibilities of the architect. Architects and clients have a far more symbiotic connection than is seen in the traditional modernist relationship, in which architectural competence and knowledge were assumed and deferred to by the client. Nevertheless, there was plenty of cross-pollination between Japanese architects and the West, particularly through publications in the 1960s and 1970s, when the work of architects such as Tadao Ando, Toyo Ito, and Kenzo Tange was given admiring critical attention. On the one hand, the new Japanese architecture was thrillingly ambitious and grandiose, but on the other the small Japanese house demonstrated a minimal creativity that was unmatched in other architectural cultures. The megastructural visions of the Metabolist movement used Tokyo as a generative force, creating a concrete utopianism that is encapsulated by Tange's 1960 plan for Tokyo Bay, featuring giant concrete piers striding across the waters to extend the city into nature. In stark contrast, the Japanese house has a very singular purpose: to facilitate and enhance a life.

Modern Tokyo can be seen as a low-rise cityscape of spectacular complexity, with the slender corporate HQs and showrooms of Ginza, for example, displaying intensively wrought detailing and material expression, all in the name of big brand recognition. The city's core population had risen to 10 million by 1960 and 13.6 million in 2017, with the Greater Tokyo area home to nearly 38 million people—one of the largest urban agglomerations in the world. Given such numbers, the cult of individualism demonstrated by the best of the city's architecture stands out, but is still in a tiny minority. Like every other

1 The Nakagin Capsule Tower in Shimbashi, Tokyo, was designed by Kisho Kurokawa and completed in 1972. It is an enduring symbol of technology-led modern design.   2 Tokyo's many low-rise residential districts are densely planned.

Industrialized nation, Japan suffers from cultural homogeneity, with an embedded work culture that marginalizes traditional domesticity and can be isolating, especially in the heart of such a colossal megacity.

Scale has given rise to ingenuity, as architects and their clients seek to fill every last scrap of available space. Gaps in the city are becoming few and far between, and architects are becoming more adept at filling them with livable, albeit very compact, designs. Space standards that would be culturally unacceptable in the United States and many parts of Europe are seen as entirely acceptable in Japan. In recent years, the increasing pressure on urban space has led to architects fusing the office with the home, further shifting what were already blurred boundaries in a city known for its high land prices and relatively small living areas. As a result, the Tokyo house continues to be an inspiration for a younger generation, in Japan and elsewhere, for whom the craft, variety, and sheer dynamism of domestic building offer a different way of thinking. Every individually designed private house is a utopian project, regardless of where it is in the world. Tokyo offers a different take on the modern city.

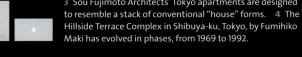

3 Sou Fujimoto Architects' Tokyo apartments are designed to resemble a stack of conventional "house" forms.   4 The Hillside Terrace Complex in Shibuya-ku, Tokyo, by Fumihiko Maki has evolved in phases, from 1969 to 1992.

TOKYO
COUNTRY Japan
ARCHITECT Elding Oscarson YEAR 2015

1 A decked roof terrace sits atop Nerima House, offering views toward the Tokyo skyline. 2 Created on the site of a small garden, this timber-clad house was designed to be respectful of the nature around it.

NERIMA HOUSE

In dense urban Tokyo, space is always at a premium. The Japanese capital has long been known for its wealth of compact, flexible, and often rather unexpected residential designs, the result of the efforts of various local architects to make new-build, single-family residences, and independent living possible in a bustling, packed, and expensive metropolis, where creative thinking can take you a long way when it comes to architectural solutions. Consequently, when a forgotten parcel of land is uncovered and becomes available for development, it is cause for great excitement, and opportunities swiftly open up.

In a modest plot in the city's verdant outskirts, a little garden had been thriving in a wild state, around an equally small old house. When Swedish architecture firm Elding Oscarson—headed by Jonas Elding and Johan Oscarson—were called upon to design a family home for this site, a key requirement of the brief stated that they needed to make sure this tiny patch of greenery was retained and allowed to grow freely and naturally around the new building.

Nerima House, a timber-clad structure, was a commission from a couple who at the time lived outside Tokyo and were planning to use the residence as a weekend home—with a view to eventually moving there permanently over the next few years. Provisions needed to be made for a parking space within the plot, and also some spare room to accommodate guests and overnight visitors, for when the couple's grown-up children joined them.

Instead of creating a house with many smaller rooms, in order to fulfill all of the client's requests, the architects decided to design only a few larger spaces, which would be open plan and as flexible as possible. The interior spans a compact 1,173 square feet (109 sq m), yet this expert move succeeded in fitting in everything comfortably, while still achieving a sense of space and lightness.

The slightly sunken ground floor contains the master bedroom, along with a bathroom and copious storage and facility rooms; its windows are on the same level as the garden, which greets the owners each morning when they draw open their curtains. A long strip window wraps around the whole volume, creating uninterrupted views out—both on this level and on the first floor, where the house's common areas sit. The integrated living, kitchen, and dining room is a generous open space, decorated in natural and light tones. When lit from all angles, it becomes pleasantly bright. Its constant visual connection to the garden creates a sense of being almost outdoors, and its high ceilings underline this airy feel.

When viewed from the outside, the strips of glazing expertly break up the timber-wrapped volume, making the structure appear light. Slender, white steel columns support the whole. They are just fine enough to not take away from the overall effect of transparency and lightness. An accessible decked terrace and roof garden crown the top. This level offers a 360-degree panorama of the site across the treetops and toward the city beyond.

3 The architects were briefed to retain the greenery already on site. 4 Inside, Japanese aesthetics meet Nordic minimalism in a wood-lined interior and neutral palette.
5 A strip window wraps around the house's cubic volume.

R·TORSO·C HOUSE

Tokyo's private housing is characterized by its economy of space and inventiveness of form. Occupying a site measuring only 710 square feet (66 sq m), R·Torso·C House by Atelier Tekuto perfectly illustrates this approach. The clients' primary request was for exposed concrete, inside and out, and the architects were chosen because Atelier Tekuto has extensive experience designing with the material and exploring new ways of forming it.

In order to maximize the sense of being open and light-filled in such a dense environment, the architects decided to make the most of the house's connection with the sky. The two-and-a-half-year design and material experimentation process focused on angling the walls of the concrete structure to emphasize the verticality of the space, with corners "pruned" away from a concrete box to form a chamfered angular object that is as much sculpture as house. Arranged over four stories, the house feels light and spacious despite its small footprint. The use of raw concrete inside and out extends the sense of space by blending floors with walls and ceilings into seamless surfaces. The elegantly simple cantilevered concrete staircase allows light to filter down into the lower levels, while the large triangular window floods the small upper-floor living space with light. The combination of high ceilings and natural lighting assists the flow of space, which runs from the sound-proofed AV room in the basement through to the gallery and traditional Japanese room on the first floor. The main living room, with its 16-foot (5 m) high ceiling, is on the second floor alongside the kitchen, dining room, and bathroom, with a bedroom occupying a mezzanine space above it.

Atelier Tekuto describe their design approach in three key methods: NU-KE, or the process of increasing the sense of space through layered walls and rising volumes; a "simultaneous contemplation of plan and section" that allows the house to be a consistent whole; and the use of a pared-back palette of color and

1 The kitchen is a cave-like recess set against the concrete walls.   2 A chamfered concrete box, the house makes a strong statement on its corner site.   3 Traditional Japanese elements are paired with meticulously finished concrete.

texture. Alongside the concrete, other key materials include charcoal-stained wood, hammered steel, and oxidized black silver plate.

The concrete is of particular interest. Developed by the architects, professors, and private companies it is 100 percent recyclable thanks to the use of "shirasu," the deposit created by volcanic pyroclastic flows, a natural material that is found in abundance in the southern parts of Japan together with limestone aggregate. Despite not using conventional sand, the shirasu concrete is extremely strong, with the natural pozzolanic reaction in the material bonding it more and more as it ages, much like the original Roman "concrete." The fineness of shirasu enables concrete to be smooth on the surface and, as R·Torso·C House demonstrates, beautifully detailed.

4 Large triangular windows are set into the towering concrete walls.   5 The master bedroom sits on a mezzanine level.

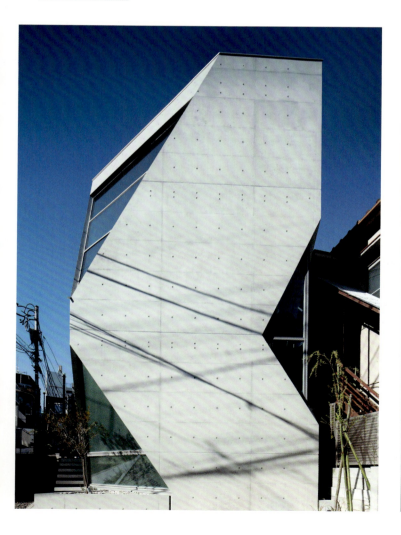

1 The views are inwardly in this small suburban house, leaving a clear external facade. **2** The main living space opens up onto the substantial covered terrace at first-floor level.

LITTLE HOUSE BIG TERRACE

Tokyo's renowned density often leaves little room for external spaces. Takuro Yamamoto's Little House Big Terrace is a piece of urban design that sets out to upend this situation. "Throughout the process of designing this house, we tried to prove that having rich private external space was important for making crucial differences in the quality of life inside the house, as well as obtaining various possibilities of external activity," says Yamamoto. The house is, therefore, configured as a volume containing both inside and outside spaces, the "big terrace" of its title. The covered terrace area adjoins a glazed three-story facade, with the house's other windows reduced in size and frequency. This not only created a sense of private enclosure, but also helped keep the budget down.

The house is arranged over four stories. At ground-floor level, there is a car port and self-contained bedroom suite, with a half-story storage space inserted above and accessed from the stair that winds around the corner of the square plan. The main living area is at second-floor level, set alongside the large terrace. The master bedroom, with adjoining study, is set on the uppermost floor, with a window overlooking the covered terrace. Thanks to the alignment of a neighboring house, the second-floor terrace still receives direct sunlight, making it a surprisingly open and airy place in a very dense part of the city, without compromising the privacy the clients desired. Oak flooring is used throughout, with open-tread stairs and a minimal steel balustrade.

The first-floor "attic" takes the pressure off storage space in the rest of the house, allowing the living space to be pushed to the envelope. A sliding section of staircase provides access. With a ceiling height of only 4½ feet (140 cm), the attic is not a habitable space, but the additional height enables the living room to be higher off the ground and therefore receive more light and privacy.

1

2

1 This multigenerational home, designed for an extended family, is nestled in a generous plot on the outskirts of Ahmedabad.   2 The contemporary interior combines raw concrete with different stones and marbles.

MOVING LANDSCAPES

Ahmedabad may be internationally renowned for its prized selection of modernist treasures, which include public works and housing by Le Corbusier, Louis Kahn, and Balkrishna Doshi, but a new generation of architects has also been quietly thriving in this Indian town. Their joint portfolio includes a rich selection of contemporary residential examples and, among them, the work of Matharoo Associates—led by Gurjit Singh Matharoo—clearly stands out for its bold designs that draw on the region's cultural and climatic conditions.

Following India's tradition for multigenerational living, this villa on the outskirts of Ahmedabad was designed for an extended family: a husband and wife, their sons, their families, and other visiting family members. The structure sits on a large plot, together with the houses of the owner's two brothers and their respective families. Titled Moving Landscapes, the house takes its name from its striking use of a very remarkable marble, Bidasar Forest. This type

of stone "possesses an impression, as if of tropical arid landscape fossilized within itself," explain the architects. The practice drew on the qualities of the stone to create a spatial play that blurs the lines between reality and illusion.

Creating a multigenerational home has its challenges. Although it is vital—and a core element of the set-up—for the family members to have their own space to withdraw to should they need to, it is equally important to design common areas and circulation in a way that does not isolate the house's residents, while still providing privacy. Conceived as a "linear pavilion," Moving Landscapes is, in its essence, a complex of three two-story volumes, arranged in a U-shape. The central part houses the common rooms for gathering and socializing: formal and informal living rooms and lounges, kitchen and dining spaces, and a gym. The two pavilions flanking it include the seven bedrooms, all with en suite bathrooms and walk-in wardrobes.

All the spaces are carefully and luxuriously designed in a combination of marble, stone, glass, and board-form naked concrete. However, the project's real centerpiece is its solid Bidasar-stone operable wall system. This impregnable floor-to-ceiling layer cocoons the "precious" interior, protecting it from the intense Gujarati heat and harsh sun. Behind this, all the internal walls are made of a continuous and uninterrupted curtain of glass, supported by a thick concrete wall on the other side. They overlook the large planted courtyard at the heart of the house, when the stone panels are open. This layer of stone panels also creates a semi-open-air buffer space that doubles up as a series of passages, veranda,s and breakout areas for the rooms on the other side. Its existence also helps with natural air circulation.

Decorated with international pieces and bespoke elements created by the architects, Moving Landscapes is a sculptural feat in residential design. Its polished materials, strips of glass, and water elements on various parts of the outdoor areas create reflections and optical illusions, which are highlighted further by the movable nature of the stone walls. All these elements make walking through this house a truly rich experience.

3 A series of movable elements clad in Bidasar stone lends the house its name. 4 A corridor supports natural ventilation and creates a cool circulation system during the region's hot months.

JAMMU

COUNTRY India
ARCHITECT Sameep Padora **YEAR** 2015

LATTICE HOUSE

Set in a new suburb of Jammu, a city of around half a million inhabitants in the far northwest of India, Lattice House is a generous family home that strives to make the most of the relatively *ad hoc* rapid urbanization that now characterizes the Indian landscape. Without formal planning requirements or official intervention, the house is designed by Mumbai-based architect Sameep Padora to be a distinct marker in the neighborhood, standing in contrast to surrounding structures with a clearly defined materiality and form, as well giving an imposing, secure presence on the street.

The dominant material is wood, which has been used to create a vertical lattice screen that envelopes the entire rectangular facade, and gives the house its name. Lattice House is shaped like an inverted ziggurat, with each successive story slightly overhanging the one below, thus helping to shade the lower levels. In addition to defining the massing of the house, the lattice facade is another response to the local climate. The region is hot and dry for around two-thirds of the year and the screening keeps the interior core of the house cool. It also simplifies the elevations and disguises the internal functions, including the services at roof level.

The plan was designed around the clients' love of entertaining. One half of the overall floor area of around 6,460 square feet (600 sq m) is given over to grand bedroom suites; the other half to a large salon with doors that open onto a slim private terrace and lawn. In fact, all the interior spaces open up to the exterior, allowing the house to be naturally ventilated when conditions permit. The combination of wooden lattice and glazed walls creates a lantern-like effect at night, and the house glows from within. Himalayan cedar wood is also used for the glazing and facade structure, creating a simple unified palette along with the marble floors. Used mainly as a second home, the uppermost level was designed to be rented out as a separate unit.

1 At night, the house glows from within like a lantern. 2 The screens form a key part of the aesthetic. 3 The shrouded structure stands out during the day. Overleaf The lattice creates a stark contrast with the *ad hoc* surroundings.

LAYERED HOUSE

The townhouse was originally a symbol of status, an easily understood composition that could convey all manner of social cues, both subtle and unsubtle. Modern cities the world over present a very different environment, and contemporary urban housing has evolved to reflect these changes. This five-bedroom family home in Colombo, designed by KWA Architects, is generously sized and contains an annex for visiting relatives as well as garaging. Yet, as its name suggests, Layered House presents a mysterious facade to the outside world. Located in a busy part of the city on a relatively small site, the house is designed to shield its occupants from the world outside, with an internal landscape of terraces and courtyards around the living accommodation.

The architects describe the house as a "three-dimensional composition of spaces layered both vertically and in plan." Outside space is limited, and although the rear garden is compact, it is beautifully landscaped and supplemented by two terraces, two courtyards, and a covered veranda at second-floor level. At ground floor, the visitor is struck first by the two timber screens that run the full width of the facade and by the large four-car garage. A tall slot on the right-hand side conceals the entrance pathway, a covered double-height space that takes you into the heart of the floor plan, past a rectangular courtyard (off which there is access to the guest and staff accommodation) and through to the main reception space overlooking the garden.

An open-plan living and dining area occupies the full width of the ground floor, with a double-height glazed wall facing a generous sweep of tropical planting. Above the kitchen space is a mezzanine, containing a living room and an enclosed study that allows the family to stay within close proximity of each other within their own spaces. The first floor also features three of the house's five bedrooms, all of which are en suite.

1 Arranged as a series of layered spaces, both vertical and horizontal, the house presents a mysterious front to the world.   2 The internal entrance courtyard reveals the structure's many different levels.

The design of Layered House takes special care to include suitable planting, with the tropical evergreen *Murraya paniculata* in the entrance courtyard and a selection of local fruit trees in the main garden. On the two upper terraces, there is space given over to a small vegetable garden and orchard, and there is also a large solar-panel array to provide power for cooling the house in the hot summers and to heat the water. The location of the two ground-floor courtyards, partially paved in old brick, creates passive ventilation for the whole structure. Despite its forbidding and enclosed appearance, Layered House presents a light and airy refuge from city noise and heat.

3 Different materials provide contrasting areas, such as this glazed garden facade.   4 White walls reference classic modernist design.   5 The kitchen and dining room have a family room on the mezzanine above.

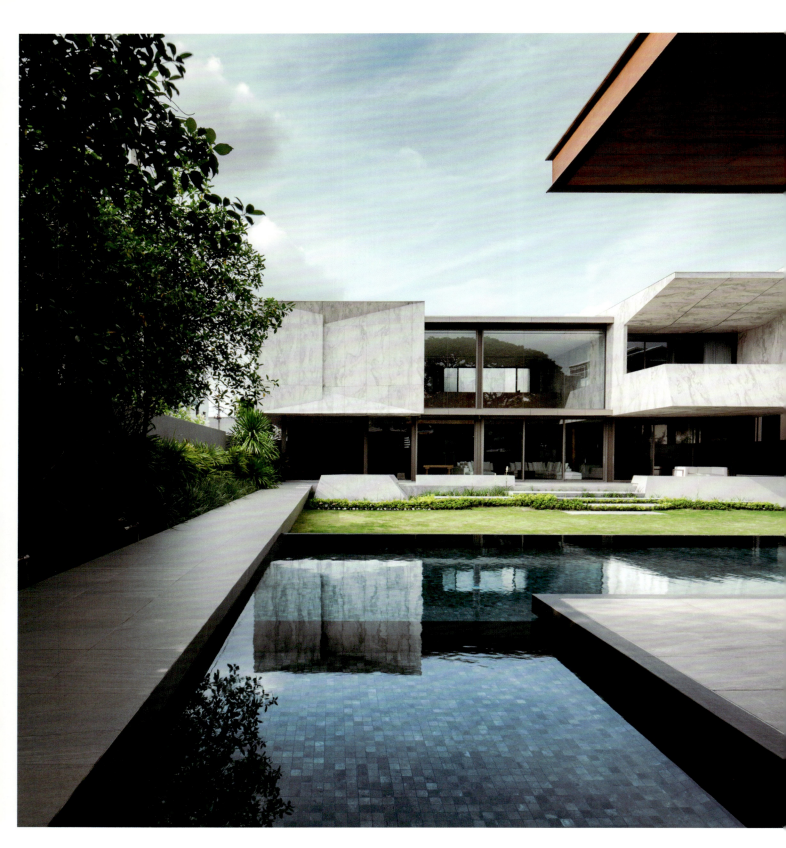

MARBLE HOUSE

Tropical modernism in architecture often conjures up images of low, raw concrete boxes, long strip windows and open-plan, dark timber-clad living spaces that merge with gardens filled with rich foliage—not with this house by Thai studio Openbox Architects. Taking their commission for a family house in an entirely different direction, husband and wife team Nui Ratiwat Suwannatrai and Prang Wannaporn Suwannatrai opted for a design that treats the house as a marble sculpture.

Located in the Thai capital of Bangkok, the project elegantly mixes architecture and landscape design in a unified approach, which is only fitting coming from a team comprising an architect (Nui) and a landscape designer (Prang). By cladding the top floor of this two-level volume in white marble, while keeping the base opaque, discreet, and comparatively dark, they created a project that feels expressive and solid, yet at the same time it appears to float lightly above ground. Marble elements can also be found strategically plotted on various spots in the garden, artfully linking this level with the building's main body above.

The two-level structure sits on one end of a rectangular plot, with a mature rain tree and a small glass-enclosed pavilion at the opposite end. An L-shaped pool between them bridges the two ends through reflections in the water. Marble House may appear solid, but bulky and awkward it is not. Its highly articulated floor plan generates several small courtyards and private terraces on both floors, which avoid being overlooked by the neighboring houses through clever massing arrangements. Windows, especially the ones facing the street, are also designed to protect the residents from views in.

The generous open-plan kitchen, living and dining areas, as well as the more secluded service rooms and staff quarters, sit on the ground floor and lead out to the various clearings outside and the garden beyond. Upstairs are the house's three bedrooms, complete with en suite bathrooms and walk-in wardrobes, as well

1 This contemporary marble-clad home may appear opaque from the street side, but it opens up toward the garden and pool at the rear of the plot.

as a family sitting room. The upper-level balconies expertly merge indoors and outdoors, while the large expanses of glass toward the garden provide a contrast to the house's seemingly closed-off street-side character, allowing the eye to travel out to the greenery and the blue skies above. Marble House's signature smooth surfaces continue inside, matched with tactile light wood floors, window frames, and detailing. Helping to produce a space that feels at the same time modern and timeless, simple and luxurious, marble is not only the result of its creators' architectural whim, it is also a key tool that keeps temperatures down and protects the house's residents from the intense Thai summer heat.

2 Three bedrooms occupy the top floor. 3 Balconies and openings ensure all the upstairs rooms remain effortlessly connected to the outdoors. 4 Inside, marble is matched by timber floors and cladding to create a warm interior.

5 The Marble House exterior appears to float, while
external landscape space flows underneath.

HO CHI MINH CITY

As is the case with many major Asian urban hubs, Ho Chi Minh City (aka HCMC, aka Saigon) is going through a golden period of reinvention. Making the most of a stint of long-awaited political stability, a young and increasingly affluent population, a flood of local and foreign investment, and plenty of history and cultural heritage to show off to the world, this Vietnamese city is having a moment—and architecture is right at the forefront. Pale yellow heritage buildings sit next to a flourishing construction industry and a growing cityscape of ultramodern skyscrapers. Vietnam is among the region's most dynamic economies and just a glance at HCMC's skyline confirms this.

Although Hanoi is the country's capital, HCMC is without doubt Vietnam's beating economic heart. Home to much of the country's industry, including sectors such as mining, agriculture, construction, tourism, and finance, HCMC is not short of investment, which means that plenty of new private and public projects and building sites now dot this city. This increased activity in many different areas resulted in a flourishing job market, which in turn inevitably led to the city's rapid population growth of the past decade.

Reflected onto the urban realm, this growth fueled the creation of whole new districts to accommodate the rush of immigration, highlighting at the same time the need for improved infrastructure to support the increasing population's daily movement and services. Entirely new or revitalized neighborhoods such as Thu Thiem and Phu My Hung are key examples, comprising a mix of commercial, residential, and public spaces. These, and other large chunks of HCMC, are currently in construction, expanding, modernizing, and priming the city to become one of the world's key metropoles. Indeed, many predict Vietnam will soon be rivaling China, especially when it comes to production power, and HCMC and its already strong industrial output would be at the center of this activity.

These large-scale changes are happening rapidly, but they are affecting mostly the city's suburbs and outer zones. Meanwhile, the city's core remains largely unchanged, and this is where many of the best townhouses can be found. Much of the center's housing is made up of Vietnam's distinctive thin, single-family dwellings. These represent a large part of the city's historic fabric, and they are known as tube houses, defined by their narrow, yet tall and long forms, which appear to unfold in a seemingly endless rear extension. It is widely claimed this was the result of a government taxation policy of the past, whereby tax was calculated according to facade width.

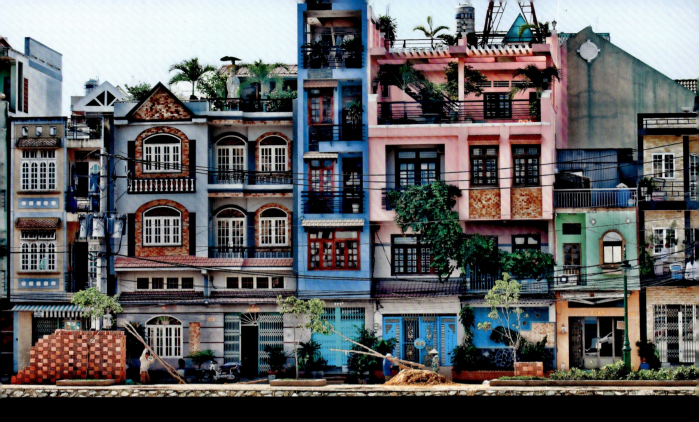

tightly packed, and typically reaching three stories, these houses are usually found in the inner-city neighborhoods. They often play host to more than one generation under one roof, as multigenerational living and an expanded family unit are common themes in the structure of Vietnamese society.

The traditional shophouse is a popular building typology in Southeast Asia, and its Vietnamese equivalent—a version of the tube house—is regularly used in HCMC, uniting residential and commercial elements in a house-above-a-shop arrangement. Influences from the country's former life as a European colony and from neighboring countries have also impacted the housing stock, resulting in several examples of both Chinese- and French-inspired houses, for example.

HCMC's burgeoning architecture scene includes many emerging and smaller practices that cut their teeth on residential commissions: examples include Block Architects, MM++ Architects, and Sanuki Daisuke Architects. Well-known foreign names, such as Japanese architect Ryue Nishizawa, are also starting to enter the field. That is not to say that larger or more well-known local practices would miss the chance to experiment with residential typologies. Rising stars include locally based Vo Trong Nghia, who works with a sustainable

1 Rapid urbanization in recent years has meant that whole new neighborhoods have been created in Ho Chi Minh City to accommodate the population growth.   2 The city's distinctive tall, narrow, and tightly packed townhouses are known as tube houses. Often they are a variation of the traditional Southeast Asian shophouse typology.

approach, plants and local materials (namely bamboo) to create modern forms and contemporary versions of what traditional Vietnamese construction techniques can deliver. A sensitive and site-specific approach such as this seems vital and timely in terms of redefining the city's residential realm. Examples such as Vo Trong Nghia's House for Trees, a composition of rectangular volumes with planted roofs that feature mature trees, highlight a welcome trend for more and better green pockets for the city.

Managing an intense pace of development and the current wave of urbanization while boosting the city's green spaces and environmentally friendly homes, and also respecting the local character and traditions, seems to be a key priority for the residential landscape. Yet, these are challenges about which local architects seem to be well informed and proactive. Buzzing with promise and dynamism, HCMC is rapidly transforming into a contemporary metropolis and a paradigm for context-sensitive urban houses, while looking at even more exciting times ahead.

3 Many of the city's young and dynamic contemporary architecture practices incorporate outdoor areas and green space in their new projects, to balance the city's densely built urban fabric.   4 Tube houses feature a long and narrow footprint that extends toward the rear. They form a large part of the city's historic housing stock, although there are also numerous modern examples and adaptations.

HO CHI MINH CITY

COUNTRY Vietnam
ARCHITECT VTN Architects and Sanuki + Nishizawa Architects   YEAR 2013

1 This project features a facade made of perforated concrete blocks; it both supports natural ventilation and filters sunlight in.   2 The house brings three generations together under one roof.

BINH THANH HOUSE

Often a house can be designed with more than a single client in mind, when, for example, it involves an extended or multigenerational family. Binh Thanh House demonstrates this approach with aplomb. Designed, in effect, for two families, this project involved a couple in their sixties and their son's family, which comprised husband, wife and a small child. Commissioned as a collaboration between Vo Trong Nghia, and his team at VTN Architects, and Sanuki + Nishizawa Architects, the house is situated on a bilateral plot in the Binh Thanh district of Ho Chi Minh City.

In addition to uniting three generations of one family, the house was required to bridge a variety of different needs and desires: although Binh Thanh House is set on a noisy and dusty street, the clients still wanted to maintain a connection to the outdoors, as the plot is located near the city's river and the greenery of Saigon Zoo. At the same time, they requested a structure that not only responds to the requirements of a traditional, low tech, indoor/outdoor lifestyle befitting a tropical climate, but also one that has

provisions for modern facilities and mechanical equipment, such as air-conditioning systems. The architects' solution revolved around alternating volumes between high- and low-tech spaces. Modern needs are addressed in the patterned concrete block-wrapped parts, while in between the team slotted airy levels that are open to the elements and cooled by natural ventilation and water. The former contain bathrooms, service rooms, and generally areas of the house where privacy requirements are higher. The latter house the common areas and living spaces.

By shifting these different volumes a little so they are not vertically flush with each other, the design not only marks them visually as separate but also helps to create various terraces throughout the building. One of the bedroom hubs is located on the semi-sunken ground floor, and the second on the very top, while the house's generous living, dining, and sitting areas are sandwiched in the middle levels, linked together by a sculptural spiral staircase in rough concrete.

The facade blocks, which are a nod to traditional breeze-block techniques of Vietnam, allow for plenty of natural ventilation and are made in precast concrete. By employing this feature, the architects manage, in a single move, to encourage air to travel through the building, to filter the region's often-harsh sunlight, to protect the open areas against heavy rain and to keep the family's inner workings away from the prying eyes of passers-by on the street level. At the same time, the perforated nature of the facade makes Binh Thanh House beam beautifully like a lantern at night, when lit from within.

Re-imagining tropical living for the twenty-first century by adding modern twists and contemporary know-how, VTN Architects and Sanuki + Nishizawa Architects created a house that not only responds perfectly to their client's needs, but also feels right at home in its bustling Ho Chi Minh City street, serving as an example of contemporary Vietnamese architecture.

3   The top level hosts some of the family bedrooms.
4   The precast concrete blocks allow long views out, but also protect the residents from prying eyes.   5   A sculptural staircase in naked concrete leads up to the living spaces.

MICRO TOWN HOUSE

Located in Ho Chi Minh City's Phú Nhuận District, Micro Town House is an attempt to revitalize the traditional housing archetype of the region, applying contemporary materials and detailing to make dense yet livable urban dwellings. Architectural firm MM++ notes that many of Ho Chi Minh City's residents are increasingly rejecting the city's narrow streets and alleyways, known as "Hẻm," in favor of living in modern apartment complexes. "Hẻm are a vital component of Ho Chi Minh City's street network and the social life of the city's inhabitants," says Mỹ An Phạm Thị, who founded Mimya (MM++ Architects) in 2009. By applying their ideas to a small urban site, the architects hope to create a new model for private housing in the inner city.

Micro Town House accommodates a family of four across four floor levels plus a terrace with rooftop views. It sits on an irregularly shaped plot of around 13 by 26 feet (4 x 8 m), formed by the *ad hoc* growth of Ho Chi Minh City's urban pattern. The result is a house that adopts the tall, narrow footprint of the city's traditional housing stock yet uses a very contemporary palette. The front facade is dominated by a vertical timber screen to provide privacy as well as a striking street presence.

The site's unusual shape allows for the creation of a small balcony and courtyard area at ground-floor and mezzanine level, above which is the overhanging upper two floors of accommodation. As the architect notes, "The site is surrounded by disparate constructions and the environment is visually chaotic," so the plain, faceted white walls, with their scattered pattern of light bricks illuminating the stairwell, stand in stark and sober contrast. Each floor of accommodation measures only around 345 square feet (32 sq m), and the challenge was to bring natural light and cross ventilation into the tall space without compromising the functionality and usability of the interior areas. The result is a house that appears to have grown organically out of a densely layered streetscape.

1 Behind the gate lies a double-height entrance hallway.   2 Tucked away in Ho Chi Minh City's narrow network of streets, Micro Town House makes the most of its small site.

1 The perforated concrete skin protects a generous
open-plan living area that leads out to a covered terrace
and pool.   2 Tropical Box is located within a leafy
residential enclave, surrounded by treetops.

TROPICAL BOX

Architects' responses to the challenges of building for a tropical climate have been imaginative and diverse: tall timber structures that peek above the canopy of rainforests; low concrete boxes that open up to lush gardens and water features; and breeze-block screen compositions. Geographical locations may vary, but the winning approach always includes finding the right balance between embracing the surrounding environment and protecting users from the tropics' heat, sun, and rain. This house ticks all the right boxes.

Situated within a leafy natural enclave of the Malaysian capital, this family home was envisioned as an inward-looking structure. The design gesture that defines it is the house's "egg-crate" concrete outer layer. This perforated skin has been wrapped around a generous interior, protecting the open-plan living spaces while allowing air and light in. This means that the house has natural air circulation and a soft light filtering through, making for a comfortable atmosphere in all seasons and weather conditions. The device also allows the house's leafy surroundings to grow and find their way around and into the structure, softening the boundaries between natural and man-made.

The house is spread across three main levels. Because of the plot's sloped nature, most of the living spaces have been raised from the ground, level with the site's treetops. Orchestrating the sequence of rooms for maximum impact, the architects lead the visitor into the house through a relatively narrow entrance lobby and corridor. The house unfolds slowly, before reaching the living room and pool area's dramatic openness. The top floor is where the bedrooms and bathrooms sit, surrounded by windows that have been carefully positioned to frame specific views. Touching the ground lightly while being connected with its environment, this is a house that is in sync with its context, providing the perfect balance between solid and transparent, light and heavy, open and protected.

SINGAPORE

Diverse and dynamic, the architecture of Singapore aptly reflects the young nation's history and cultural makeup. This small but perfectly formed city-state sits on an island on the southern tip of the Malay Peninsula and has only been a sovereign nation since 1965. However, a young and ambitious population that enjoys sampling the finer things in life, a healthy economy, and a reasonably long stretch of political stability have, within a few decades, transformed this enterprising Asian nation into a hotbed of architectural production.

In the century up to the end of the 1950s, Singapore was a British colony. In 1963, it declared its independence and began its journey to what we now know as the Republic of Singapore: an international, multicultural financial powerhouse, where streets are squeaky clean and smelly durians are banned from the subway. Education, healthcare, life expectancy, quality of life, personal safety, and housing are all thriving in this tropical corner of the world—good news for the construction sector, which has been steadily flourishing.

Singapore may be tiny compared to its neighbors, but when it comes to money and culture, it can really pack a punch. This country has not only the strongest economy in the region, but one of the strongest in the world, priding itself on its innovative and business-friendly market. This helped to inject significant funding into the creative industries, and the country has now become a key player in the Asian fine-art market, with design following hot on its heels. The city's cultural cachet rose even further with the opening of the revamped National Gallery in 2015, designed by French architecture firm Studio Milou in partnership with locals CPG Consultants. Meanwhile, large-scale projects in the sports and leisure industries, such as the Sports Hub by the Kallang River and Gardens by the Bay, have been highlighting the country as a major tourist destination.

It was only a matter of time before residential architecture followed suit, and with an affluent middle class ready to sink a healthy chunk of its capital into the market (the country has been considered by many a safe haven and a wise investment), Singapore features a wide selection of quality housing to boot. The country's well-preserved and varied housing stock and its sociopolitical and economic conditions made this little patch of land in the Straits a very attractive proposition for investors in the noughties. This resulted in a huge jump in prices and soaring land values, making Singapore one of the most coveted places to own land in Asia. Now, mostly due to government restrictions on mortgages, the market has stabilized.

Like its population and its famously celebrated food scene, Singapore's architecture is anything but homogenous. The urban realm is made up of different styles and periods, from local traditional

structures through to colonial and contemporary buildings. The
housing ranges from colonial villas such as the famous—and, now,
pretty rare—black-and-white bungalows to Chinese shophouses and
homes that draw on the local vernacular.

There are contemporary examples, too, although empty lots and
new-build houses are quickly becoming scarce, as land is far from
limitless and nowadays comes at a premium. There are small pockets
of lower-rise residential neighborhoods spread across town, and
that is where most of the city's modern townhouses can be found.
They are often designed to embrace the region's warm climate and
abundant sunshine, featuring a seamless connection of indoors
and outdoors, and lush tropical gardens and water features.

At the opposite end of the spectrum, at least in terms of size, are
Singapore's signature public housing blocks. Large-scale multifamily
structures began emerging everywhere on the island from 1959,
when the People's Action Party came to power and embarked
on tackling the young country's housing crisis. Built in a mix of
International Style, Brutalist, and Art Deco architecture, these
projects were conceived to house the nation's growing middle classes,
and quickly became instrumental in defining Singapore's urban

1 A rich mix of architectural styles and housing
typologies reflect Singapore's diverse population
and history.   2 The rare black-and-white villas
are part of the country's colonial heritage.

realm. Large, often concrete, developments, such as Tiong Bahru, now dot the capital, relieving the housing shortage with their typical range of two- and three-bedroom apartments. This is where many of Singapore's well-to-do still live.

The existing public housing stock is now being enriched by a number of new residential schemes, both public and private, that have slowly been transforming whole areas and creating new neighborhoods as a result of the recent building boom. The Interlace, a striking twenty-four-story development in the Southern Ridges, designed by Ole Scheeren, is one such an example, weaving eye-catching architecture with sustainability, green common spaces, and generous and light-filled apartment interiors. Studio Daniel Libeskind's Reflections at Keppel Bay is another example, while Zaha Hadid Architects, UNstudio, Jean Nouvel, and Moshe Safdie have all also worked on signature housing projects here.

3 The small country is experiencing steady growth, with many architects—both local and international—building new housing there. Completed in 2013, The Interlace by Ole Scheeren is one of the latest additions.   4 Studio Daniel Libeskind's Reflections at Keppel Bay is another new large-scale residential development, whose contemporary shapes have come to define its neighborhood.

SINGAPORE
COUNTRY Singapore
ARCHITECT Hyla Architects   YEAR 2014

LINES OF LIGHT HOUSE

Modest private houses are relatively rare on the ground in Singapore. As in many major Asian cities, the most common form of housing is the apartment building, with government-built blocks joined by signature projects by private developers. The focus is almost always on density. Individual houses were traditionally built only for the very affluent and as a result tend to be restricted to certain low-rise areas. Smaller row houses are slightly more common, but by far the most coveted housing archetype in the city is the grand detached villa.

Lines of Light House is an attempt to bring the sense of scale and vision of the villa to a relatively dense low-rise neighborhood. Occupying a corner site with a westerly orientation, the design is arranged to screen the interior from excessive solar gain. This takes the form of a recessed glass facade beneath an extruded roof pitch, which provided a covered terrace as well as the required shade.

Although the exterior forms are uncompromisingly modern, geometric, and pared back, the architects drew inspiration from the local vernacular, in particular the traditional Malay kampung house, which is raised up on stilts, uses post-and-beam construction, and often has slatted timber facades for ventilation and privacy. "The house is a modern interpretation of that, with its modular steel columns and the timber screen," they say. The entire street elevation is enveloped by a wraparound slatted timber screen, with a narrow walled tropical garden acting as another buffer zone.

Inside, the house tapers to its narrowest point at the far end of the site, with all services and the staircase pushed to the edge of the plan. A double-height sitting room, kitchen, and dining area occupy the ground floor, with sliding glass doors opening up to the garden. Three bedrooms are on the floor above, with a master suite occupying the entire attic floor, along with a study, gym, generous wardrobe, and small covered terrace. The house succeeds in addressing both the edge conditions of its plot and the historical context of Singapore.

	2
1	
	3

1 The double-height living room adjoins a covered external space.   2 Lines of Light House occupies a prominent corner site, and uses screens and planting for privacy.   3 The tropical garden transforms the urban experience.

SINGAPORE
COUNTRY Singapore
ARCHITECT Park + Associates   YEAR 2014

1 The architects wrapped the front facade in a metal mesh screen, so the residents can enjoy both light-filled interiors and privacy.   2 A slim white frame matches the house's semi-transparent white powder-coated screen.

GREJA HOUSE

Singapore housing conjures up images of grand twentieth-century public developments and concrete modernist residential blocks, such as SkyVille @ Dawson and the Golden Mile Complex, yet small pockets of contemporary lower-scale private houses can also be found in this modern city-state, often tucked away within boutique, private residential enclaves. Greja House is one such example, set within a quiet unassuming residential road bordered on one side by the Bedok River. Designed by local architecture firm Park + Associates, headed by principal architect Lim Koon Park, the house was created as a celebration of the idea of the family home. It is firmly rooted to its built context and its location's climatic conditions.

Greja House spans three levels and a comfortable footprint, yet its light and transparent volumes mean that it feels anything but disproportionately big, stuffy, or solid. Hidden behind a semi-transparent white powder-coated metal mesh screen, the semidetached structure—a glass-enclosed volume wrapped around a slim white frame—is elegant and open. At the same time, its street-facing perforation ensures that the influx of natural light and urban vistas is not compromised by the views in.

The architects interpreted the internal arrangement as a smooth spatial flow, approaching the creation of rooms in an unconventional way. Instead of putting up walls to form divisions and separate functions, they chose to weave in functions and voids, allowing the latter to define the former. Circulation played an important role in this plan, and the house's striking wood-and-metal staircase, which swirls across all floors and down into a reflective pool on the ground level, becomes a key interior centerpiece. A fairly traditional layout arrangement places the open-plan living areas on the ground level, together with a secondary bedroom at the back and a parking spot at the front, while other bedrooms are located upstairs. The master

suite, including a dressing room and bathroom, spreads out to fill the entire first floor. The top level contains two more bedrooms with their own en suite bathrooms and walk-in wardrobes. Views through levels and across different parts of the house allow for uninterrupted visual connections, thus reinforcing interaction between the residents and supporting family life. Glass walls encourage a similar continuous connection with the outdoors, with the lush garden and water elements effortlessly becoming part of the internal space.

At first glance, Greja House is a simple translucent box—bright, airy, and discreet. However, a better look at its design reveals far more than that. This is a modern townhouse that expertly weaves inside and outside, as well as its different internal spaces, within a single, seamless architectural flow.

3 Generous open-plan living spaces are linked to private areas above via a dramatic staircase.   4 Extensive glazing ensures the residents can enjoy green views.   5 The views through rooms allow for visual connections and interaction.

SR HOUSE

SR House is an example of contemporary tropical modernism on a grand scale, fully exploiting the characteristics of the Jakartan climate with a very internationalist approach to form, materials, and functional arrangements. Jakarta's domestic architecture mixes the regional vernacular with influences from the colonial era. While traditional domestic design frequently uses wood and other natural materials for structure and cladding, with steeply pitched roofs that are often exaggerated for decorative and symbolic effect, the style was denigrated by colonialists, who imported a form of architecture that slowly evolved to accommodate local conditions. This included deep verandas for shading and decorative elements that incorporate both local materials and internationally acknowledged stylistic detailing, from classical columns to Art Deco-style streamlining.

The architecture of Jakarta still presents a fusion of forms, but contemporary architecture offers a broader palette for innovation. SR House is embedded in the cityscape, with an internal landscape created out of structural elements. The house is formed of two separate masses, with a master bed pavilion reached from a first-floor structural bridge. All service elements are located at ground-floor level, behind a relatively conventional street facade that does little to imply the complexity and layering of the spaces within. Access to the main house is via a walkway that slopes up through the site to an entrance foyer at first-floor level. Here the separations are obvious, with the master bedroom suite treated like a self-contained single-story pavilion, set atop the service floor. From here, there is also direct access to the lap pool and raised courtyard garden.

The main living area runs full width across the site, with a covered veranda and small courtyard garden at the far end, also overlooked by the guest suite. The floor above has two further bedroom suites and a library and office area. Staff accommodation, utility spaces, storage, and a catering kitchen are all located on the ground floor, along with a generous home cinema. A flat roof oversails the upper floor, providing space for the raised garden that fringes the bedrooms and library. The architects and designers have made extensive use of

1 The tree rises up from the ground level so its canopy becomes part of the first-floor terrace and pool area.

evergreen tropical planting, with hanging and climbing plants and trees that rise up through courtyards to unite the different levels—most notably a mature tree on the ground-floor inner court. Modern detailing and design elements such as large sliding glass doors make the most of the tropical climate. The extensive use of raw materials, including exposed concrete, gray stone, and marble, is juxtaposed with hardwood and a slender steel structure for the bridge element.

The careful massing of SR House conceals the many changes in level that occur throughout, alternating between a strong sense of connectivity with the site and a more ethereal, transparent upper section. The Indonesian climate is used as a generator for the design, shaping an interior that feels as if it is expanding into its surroundings while still offering privacy in the city.

2 The main living room is raised up above the accommodation for maximum light and privacy.
3 An entrance walkway to the right of the garage rises up to bring visitors into the heart of the house.

AUSTRALIA & NEW ZEALAND

SYDNEY MELBOURNE AUCKLAND

2 Architect Robin Boyd was one of the foremost proponents of the International Style in Australian architecture. Pictured here is the Walsh Street House in Melbourne that he designed for his family in 1957 and which continues to influence architectural thinking.

2

Talk of Australia's residential scene often conjures up idyllic images of peaceful holiday homes set within a stunning nature of long sandy beaches, uninhabited deserts, and picturesque forests. Certainly, the bush is home to some of the world's most dramatic houses: modern design, boldly placed in spectacular settings. However, despite its vast, sparsely built territories, Australia remains a highly urbanized country, with almost 90 per cent of the population living in cities. Look a little closer and it soon becomes apparent that the housing scene here is defined by the country's urban sites, and more specifically by the most dominant residential genre in Australian cities—the suburban home.

Australian contemporary architecture certainly has some roots in the native vernacular (in the employment, for example, of local materials and building techniques), but it has been heavily influenced by the country's colonial history, with European styles largely shaping the scene. Victorian, Georgian, and Regency buildings are most commonly found, but in fact the majority of the European nineteenth- and twentieth-century architecture movements are well represented in the biggest cities, such as Sydney and Melbourne. Created by immigrants who brought with them their own regional influences, knowledge, and skills, contemporary Australia is a real melting pot of cultures and house styles. This is why most cities feature a highly mixed housing stock, where humble Californian-inspired bungalows can be found side by side with spacious villas, rows of brick townhouses, and grand mansions. In order to make the most of the country's pleasant climate, fenced-off gardens and porches are a common feature in most iterations, not only feeding one of the country's most beloved stereotypes—the Australian barbecue—but also drawing on US and UK housing references.

The residential scene has indeed been affected by US influences in more ways than one. The Australian Dream of home ownership—derived from the respective 1940s American equivalent—means that Australians have always favored single-family housing over larger-scale schemes, thus leading to the sprawling suburbs of detached houses seen today. This trend has played a key part in the current high house prices. Add to this

the country's ongoing population flow toward the bigger urban hubs (kick-started by the baby boomer generation during the second half of the twentieth century), and you get modern-day Australia's residential real-estate market: diverse, growing, and one of the most expensive in the world.

This also means that residential projects of all shapes and sizes, from ground-up new builds to renovations, loft extensions, and rear additions, are the bread and butter of most architecture firms. Today, Australian houses continue to be diverse, stretching in flair and ambition from the most conventional to the most experimental, bridging traditions and influences in a blend that remains at the forefront of contemporary residential design. Firms such as Melbourne-based Austin Maynard and Inarc Architects lead the way on the scene, crafting striking homes for all plots and sizes, from humble yet thoroughly modern workers' cottage renovations to grand, modernist-inspired suburban mansions.

Queensland is another particularly prolific region architecturally, offering a wealth of examples of the Australian version of the sub-tropical modern house—all sculptural forms set within flowing lush gardens, open-plan living spaces, screens and floor-to-ceiling glazing that leads to majestic terraces and water features. This region is also the birthplace of the Queenslander house, a commonly found version of a detached, wooden single-family home with a corrugated-iron roof. It was first developed in the nineteenth century but remains popular today, both in urban centers such as Brisbane and in the countryside.

Naturally, even the suburban realm has its variations. While rows of detached houses are certainly commonplace, especially in inner-city areas, more sparsely built environments are typical in the outer, more affluent, parts of town. Plots can be so large and nature so rich that neighbors are hardly visible, making some houses feel as serene and secluded as the most remote holiday homes. This is where many of the country's modernist oeuvres can be found, such as the Rose Seidler House by Harry Seidler, one of the country's finest proponents of the International Style (although other prime examples, such as Robin Boyd's Walsh Street House, sit in slightly denser settings). Australia's only Pritzker Prize winner to date, Glenn Murcutt, also built in similar

3 Completed in 1950, the Rose Seidler House was designed by one of Australia's most important modernists, Harry Seidler. It is located in a remote bushland site of Wahroonga, a suburb of Sydney.

settings, even though he is most well known for his rural work. Back to the twenty-first century, and projects by architects such as Sydney-based Peter Stutchbury offer the contemporary version of the majestic suburban villa: nestled in generous lots, open to nature, and connected to the elements, while using bold lines and offering subtle luxury.

Australia's next-door neighbor, New Zealand, has a similarly configured residential realm, although a miniature version by comparison in both land mass and population. Its sprawling, low-density suburbs unfold from its main urban cores; here, the urban meets the country's lush nature, blurring boundaries. Many architects thrive in the design and redesign of new and existing homes, combining the local and international, and using creative ways to reach sustainable and cost-efficient solutions. The housing market, here too, is expensive, especially due to foreign interest (New Zealand is seen by many as a safe haven in case of global catastrophe, and property has often been bought by the wealthy as "insurance").

Despite a demanding market, working with an everyday typology such as the humble home, and elevating it to the next level—using inspired designs, modern materials and techniques, and a creative overall approach—architects in both countries make the most of their context, budget, and climate. And while the wider continent's other—and mostly significantly smaller—countries, such as Papua New Guinea, Fiji, and Samoa, present a similarly developed, albeit pint-sized, combination of local vernacular and European styles, when it comes to Oceania's housing stock, Australia and New Zealand no doubt lead the way in the architectural cutting edge. As a result, today both countries can boast some of the field's most respected specialists, doing their part to shape the contemporary residential scene, not only within their continent, but also internationally.

SYDNEY

When it comes to its place within the global housing market, Sydney might surprise you. The city has one of the most expensive contemporary housing markets, but when you look closely at this popular booming city—with its magnificent sandy beaches, dynamic population, vibrant foodie scene, stunning geography, and year-round sunny weather—it all starts to make sense.

The Sydney area was populated by indigenous Australians for millennia before the British transported convicts there in the late nineteenth century, slowly taking over the continent. This move also marked the birth of modern-day Sydney, in a part of the world that was described at the time by British botanist John White as the "finest and most extensive harbour in the universe". Indeed, an undulating shoreline forms a series of coves, safe ports, and friendly beaches in an enviable natural landscape, and the town quickly expanded during the twentieth century. It spread along the coast and across both sides of the bay, which are now linked by Sydney Harbour Bridge.

As the population grew, the city's architecture started to take shape. Each wave of new settlers brought their own styles and cultural references, and the city developed as a medley of European (admittedly, mostly British) influences, including Victorian, Georgian, Gothic Revival, and Neoclassical buildings. Modernist principles also made their appearance, with Austrian immigrant Harry Seidler, who became a key figure in the local architecture scene, creating a series of award-winning projects. Seidler is widely acknowledged as having introduced the International Style to the region and his work spans several typologies, including individual houses and larger-scale blocks, such as Darlinghurst's Horizon Apartments.

Sydney had reached 3 million people by the 1970s and steadily grew into a global megacity by the turn of the century, with a total population of some 5 million. At the same time, the Olympics Games of 2000 was widely hailed as one of the most successful ever. This gave Sydney the chance to shine, boosting market confidence and paving the way for bold and ambitious contemporary architecture projects in the decades to come. Today, a bird's eye view of Sydney unveils a sea of construction sites. State-of-the-art urban developments, such as Barangaroo on the northwestern edge of the Central Business District, dot this crane-filled city, where building is a booming industry; this includes residential and commercial schemes, as well as infrastructure. Signature buildings by household names in architecture, such as Richard Rogers, Jean Nouvel, Frank Gehry, and Renzo Piano, are now part of the skyline. Even more are in the pipeline, from the likes of Kengo Kuma, Grimshaw Architects, Wilkinson Eyre, 3XN, Norman Foster, and OMA.

Meanwhile, the housing stock is a reflection of Sydney's overall architectural mix. There is a bit of everything, from lower-rise residential areas such as laid-back Bondi Beach, the pretty terraced houses of Paddington and the affluent Point Piper, to higher-rise neighborhoods such as Chippendale and Parramatta, which host a denser housing and commercial blend. One thing is for certain, though; Sydneysiders love their houses. Despite the intense ongoing construction and the gradual densification of several inner-city districts, this is a residential landscape made up mostly of single-family houses, fueled by the "Australian Dream" of home ownership. There are rows of townhouses in some areas, but the urban fabric is without doubt dominated by Sydney's sprawling suburbs of detached family homes. This, combined with the country's urbanization, not enough decentralization, a growing population, and fairly limited available land in the city's central neighborhoods, has led to a large demand for housing and soaring prices in recent decades. Not that this has stopped the creative minds.

In fact, this particular residential makeup has put Sydney architects in a unique position; if you want to become a specialist in urban, single-family dwellings, this is the ideal place to be. From new

1 Harry Seidler's Horizon Apartments in Darlinghurst feature a distinctive sculptural facade made of protruding concrete balconies that jut out from the main apartment core.   2 Jean Nouvel's recently completed One Central Park is one of Chippendale's latest residential additions; it features green vertical gardens.

builds to creative renovations, extensions, additions, and restorations, Sydney offers plenty of opportunities to develop exciting, innovative architecture in the residential realm. Working with an established urban fabric and existing structures, from larger villas to bungalows and workers' cottages, is many practices' bread and butter. Creating a strong relationship between inside and outside is another recurring theme, due to the region's pleasant climate. So, open spaces, porches, and gardens, as well as visual connections to the outdoors, are a must. Although the urban context includes conventional examples, it also features bold statements and contemporary visions of Australian modernism, led by a slew of dynamic architecture practices, such as Hassell, LAVA, Welsh + Major, and Archer Office.

3 Rows of townhouses in a variety of historical styles that were imported from Europe are common in many parts of Sydney. **4** Dynamic practices such as Welsh + Major define Sydney's architectural scene, with works that include this new-build home on Albert Street.

SYDNEY
COUNTRY Australia
ARCHITECT Archer Office   YEAR 2016

BRONTE HOUSE

Extending existing structures is a traditional way of starting an architectural career, but few projects are as transformational as Bronte House. The addition to an existing semidetached brick-built bungalow in the beach-side Sydney suburb of Bronte is practically a new standalone structure. Finished in finely crafted timber, Archer Office's design vastly increases the floor space of the house by installing an extension atop the rear of the existing structure. This wood-clad box effectively turns the house from a one-bedroom property into a four-bedroom one, with a generous glass-walled, open-plan living space that makes the most of Sydney's warm climate. Like many Australian cities, Sydney has a large number of individually named suburbs—more than 550—many of which were set out in the nineteenth century. Housing stock is hugely varied, but attitudes to restoration, replacement, and radical change have ensured that the city's residential architecture is progressive and forward thinking.

Like that of many typical semidetached properties, the site of Bronte House is long and narrow. The extension pushes the amount of usable space right to the building line, while a wraparound deck integrates into the garden, helping to blur the difference between inside and outside space. The addition also had to contain a stairway, in this case a straight flight that also doubles up as storage in the open-plan kitchen area. At the rear of the house, the new first floor contains three double bedrooms, whereas the master bedroom to the front has a semi-enclosed triangular terrace (or outdoor room) formed from the former roof space of the original house. The sloping walls retain the geometry of the old pitched roof, paired with new metal railings. The contrast between original brick and timber planking, both horizontally and vertically, creates a warmth and texture to the house, inside and out. Throughout the project, the intersection of old and new is ingenious and deftly handled, adding fresh life to a small, outdated structure.

1 The new garden facade stands in complete contrast to the original bungalow.   2 A new roof terrace uses the space once occupied by the original pitched roof.   3 The separation between new and old is marked with a change in floor surface.

BALMAIN HOUSES

This set of twin houses is located in the inner Sydney suburb of Balmain and involves the transformation of two small workers' cottages into adjoining homes for different generations of the same family. The project, by award-winning, locally based architecture practice Benn & Penna, founded by Alice Penna and Andrew Benn, takes multigenerational living to a whole new level.

The two houses were designed to be similar enough for them to read as a single coherent architectural piece, but at the same time be completely independent, in order to support each resident's individual needs. The spatial composition was conceived as a sequence of "unfolding scenes," explain the architects. Rooms "bend and tilt," overlapping and merging, creating an internal narrative that takes the visitor from one space to another in a seamless motion. At the same time, careful thought has gone into ensuring that privacy is maintained where necessary. While one house features living spaces, bathroom, and master bedroom downstairs, leaving the upstairs level free for a generous workspace, the other house separates functions in a more traditional way: common areas can be found on the ground floor, and the master bedroom, bathroom, and study are nestled upstairs. These lead out to a narrow but long balcony, protected by a wooden screen.

By adding double-height volumes and opening up to the garden outside, the architects have achieved a remarkable sense of spaciousness in what is, in effect, a relatively compact site. Carefully placed openings enhance sunlight and views out, while timber shades protect the owners from prying eyes and heat. They also create a gentle play of light and shadow within the house, softening the interiors. Immaculate detailing, a considerate spatial arrangement that satisfies an unusual brief and a sophisticated balance of new and existing materials make these two fairly modest houses a true labor of architectural love.

1 One of the houses features a more traditional layout, with common areas on the ground level.   2 The living spaces open up to the garden.   3 The two houses are similar in style, but each has its own distinct identity.

MELBOURNE
COUNTRY Australia
ARCHITECT Austin Maynard Architects   YEAR 2014

1 The eclectic facade makes the house appear to be a collection of smaller structures.   2 The shingle-clad front conceals internal double-height spaces.
3 Long vistas are created through the main living spaces.

TOWER HOUSE

Tower House is the radical re-imagining of a traditional weatherboard home in the Melbourne suburb of Alphington. "As homes increase in size, they increasingly appear as hostile monoliths," the architects say. "When a home is extended, often the monolith crashes into the original." Tower House solves this dilemma by re-purposing the property as a series of smaller, interconnected structures.

The design was partly inspired by sketches and ideas drawn up by the clients' twin sons, who were invited to share their ideas for their ideal house. The end result is an eclectic piece of residential place making, a domestic space that uses esoteric abstractions of the traditional "house" to create a staggered, broken facade of multiple setbacks and protrusions. This gives the impression of a fascinating series of structures that appear to have grown organically over the years. The north elevation is especially reminiscent of this "miniature village" approach, featuring a series of pitched roofs of varying

heights to represent a scaled-down townscape. The architects describe this staggered roofscape as a "fifth facade" and note that the widespread availability of online mapping and photography is making design decisions that were once hidden visible to anyone with a computer. "With this in mind, we deliberately designed Tower House so that it looked beautiful from the sky and from Google Earth," they say.

The combination of digital picturesque with an "anti-monolithic" approach also breaks down the scale of this single-story house. For a start, the interior spaces are not intended to align with the exterior shapes, allowing for generous and unconventionally arranged rooms, such as the large open-plan kitchen/diner, as well as a long vista that stretches from the front door right through to the rear of the house. The children's bedrooms are in the "old" part of the house, with a new master bedroom and adjacent library in the new section. High ceilings

and mezzanine spaces are exploited wherever possible. This is especially visible in the children's studio and bedroom area, with a tall bookshelf and a hanging net suspended halfway up the space. In contrast, the library room is semi-submerged, with a plants-eye view of the garden.

Ultimately, Tower House was intended to create a long-term family home that can grow and be adapted as the family ages and demands and needs change. However, it also needed to be flexible from the start. Sliding panels in the walls allow for endless variations of space and privacy, while a strong sustainability program makes the most of the Australian climate to stave off solar gain and avoid the need for air-conditioning. The refurbishment has had to fulfill a complex but playful and far-reaching brief.

Tower House also serves to round off the local streetscape by slotting into a small gap between existing structures (completing the odd numbering system at the same time). Most importantly of all, the clients have used the reconstruction as an opportunity to engage with the local community by installing a communal vegetable patch and cut-throughs in the garden to unite two local streets.

4 A chill-out zone made from netting enlivens the children's area. 5 The study and library form a secluded, wood-lined space. 6 The playful shapes of the house are echoed in the kitchen cabinetry.

RED HOUSE

This eye-catching house, nestled in a pocket of New Zealand's native bush in the suburbs of Auckland, is the work of local practice Crosson Architects, which is headed by Ken Crosson.

Red House is a compact dwelling, and it was designed to be both cost- and space-efficient. However, being economical did not mean that the architects had to hold back when it came to the design. The building was conceived as a "simple abstract cube, sitting within its natural surrounds," they explain. While the relatively modest budget was a key driver in the design solution, the client's brief, which outlined a two-bedroom home with an artist's studio—the owners are a musician and an artist—and the site's lush vegetation also served as inspiration for Crosson, who approached this home as a "livable treehouse," raising it high up above the bush's low greenery.

Clever creative details and touches make this little house stand out among its peers. Its bright red corrugated-iron cladding is arranged in different placements and directions, forming a decorative pattern that also helps articulate the building's form and breaks up the overall volume. The cubic shape appears simple from the outside, but allows for maximum flexibility in the spatial arrangement inside. Linear openings, some vertical and others horizontal, running the length of the facade, open up the space to the outdoors, bringing nature effortlessly inside.

Sitting on a footprint that is as compact as it could possibly be in order to minimize the impact of the construction on the existing trees on site, the house consists of three levels: a ground floor that features two bedrooms, a bathroom and a studio gallery space; a second floor containing the main living spaces; and a third level, which consists of the roof terrace overlooking the leafy context. This acts as the residence's primary outside space. A boardwalk lined with timber planks leads up to the main entrance from the street. It cantilevers over the bush on the other end, creating a small contemplation spot—a place to pause, breath and look out toward the foliage. The interiors are lined with plywood panels, which at places fold and

1   2

1 Designed within a simple cube, this house features plenty of openings that flood the interior with natural light.   2 The house's eye-catching red skin is made from corrugated-iron cladding.

transform into shelves, cabinets, and steps, wrapping seamlessly around the residents' furniture and art. The wood makes for a warm, homely atmosphere inside, but at the same time visually connects the indoors to the trees around the house. The architects also used recycled rimu timber and black joinery—the latter "referencing the abundant native berries and ponga trees," they explain. And while adopting the somewhat industrial exterior's vivid red color proved to be a challenge when it came to obtaining planning permission, Crosson and his team eventually swam through the process. "Our argument was that if 'barn red' is part of the Waiheke Island district plan, why not in Titirangi?"

3 The interiors are fully lined in plywood panels, which transform into staircases and storage units where needed.
4 Maintaining a strong connection with the outdoors, Red House is set within a pocket of bushland.

READ UP!

INTRODUCTION

Bell, Jonathan
21st Century House
Laurence King Publishing, 2006

Bell, Jonathan and Stathaki, Ellie
The New Modern House: Redefining Functionalism
Laurence King Publishing, 2012

Boydell, Christine et al
The Modern House Revisited (Twentieth Century Architecture)
Twentieth Century Society, 2006

Le Corbusier
Towards a New Architecture (Translated by Frederick Etchells)
J. Rodker, 1931

Sudjic, Deyan
The Language of Cities
Penguin, 2017

Weston, Richard
Twentieth-Century Residential Architecture
Abbeville Press, 2004

Weston, Richard
House in the Twentieth Century
Laurence King Publishing, 2002

Yorke, F. R. S.
The Modern House.
Architectural Press (London), 1934

NORTH AMERICA

Gordon, Alastair
Weekend Utopia. Modern Living in the Hamptons
Princeton Architectural Press, 2001

Holl, Steven
Rural and Urban House Types
Princeton Architectural Press, 1996

Jenkins, Hannah
The American House: 100 Contemporary Homes
Images Publishing, 2017

Kristal, Marc
The New Old House: Historic & Modern Architecture Combined
Abrams Books, 2017

Zeiger, Mimi
Tiny Houses in the City
Rizzoli, 2016

LATIN AMERICA

Andreoli, Elisabetta and Forty, Adrian (editors)
Brazil's Modern Architecture
Phaidon Press, 2007

Anelli, Renato, et al
Lina Bo Bardi 100: Brazil's Alternative Path to Modernism
Hatje Cantz, 2014

Gestalten (editor)
Isay Weinfeld: An Architect from Brazil
Gestalten, 2018

McGuirk, Justin
Radical Cities: Across Latin America in Search of a New Architecture
Verso Books, 2014

EUROPE

Bell, Jonathan
The Modern House
Artifice, 2016

Moore, Rowan
Slow Burn City: London in the Twenty-First Century
Picador, 2017

Movement, Adam and Biles, Annabel
Infill: New Houses for Urban Sites
Laurence King Publishing, 2009

AFRICA

Adjaye, David
Adjaye · Africa · Architecture: A Photographic Survey of Metropolitan Architecture
Thames & Hudson, 2016

Fry, Maxwell and Drew, Jane
Tropical Architecture in the Humid Zone
B. T. Batsford, 1956

Herz, Manuel, et al (editors)
African Modernism: The Architecture of Independence. Ghana, Senegal, Côte d'Ivoire, Kenya, Zambia
Park Books, 2015

Koolhaas, Rem
Lagos: How It Works
Lars Muller Publishers, 2007

Taschen, Angelika (editor)
South Africa Style
Taschen, 2006

ASIA

Ciorra, Pippo and Ostende, Florence
The Japanese House: Architecture and Life after 1945
Marsilio, 2017

Jodidio, Philip
The Japanese House Reinvented
Thames & Hudson, 2017

McGillick, Paul
The Sustainable Asian House: Thailand, Malaysia, Singapore, Indonesia, Philippines
Tuttle Publishing, 2014

Pollock, Naomi
The Modern Japanese House
Phaidon, 2005

Pollock, Naomi
Jutaku: Japanese Houses
Phaidon, 2015

Souteyrat, Jérémie
Tokyo no ie: Maisons de Tokyo
Le Lézard Noir, 2014

AUSTRALIA & NEW ZEALAND

Crafti, Stephen
Architects' Houses: Twenty Australian Homes
Murdoch Books, 2015

Fromonot, Françoise
Glenn Murcutt: Building and Projects 1962–2003
Thames & Hudson, 2003

Gatley, Julia (editor)
Long Live the Modern: New Zealand's New Architecture, 1904–1984
Auckland University Press, 2009

Jackson, Davina
Next Wave: Emerging Talents in Australian Architecture
Thames & Hudson, 2007

McEoin, Ewan and Johnston, Lindsay
Under the Edge: The Architecture of Peter Stutchbury
Thames & Hudson, 2016

Murcutt, Glenn
Glenn Murcutt: Thinking Drawing/Working Drawing
Toto, 2008

INDEX

PICTURE CREDITS

(Key: t = top; b = bottom; l = left; r = right; tl = top left; tr = top right; bl = bottom left; br = bottom right)

2 © Edward Hendricks (Architect: Park + Associates); **6** © Dennis Gilbert/VIEW; **9** Arcaid Images/Alamy Stock Photo; **10** Richard Brine-VIEW/Alamy Stock Photo; **12** SuperStock/Alamy Stock Photo; **15** National Geographic Creative/Alamy Stock Photo; **16–19** © Ema Peter; **20** Nikreates/Alamy Stock Photo; **21** Torontonian/Alamy Stock Photo; **22** Roberto Machado Noa/LightRocket via Getty Images; **23** robertharding/Alamy Stock Photo; **24–25** © Borzu Talaie; **26 tl, 26 tr** © Bob Gundu; **26 b** © Colin Faulkner; **27** © Bob Gundu; **28–31** © Adrien Williams; **32** Art Kowalsky/Alamy Stock Photo; **33** Terry Smith Images/Alamy Stock Photo; **34** UrbanTexture/Alamy Stock Photo; **35** Aerial Archives/Alamy Stock Photo; **36–39** © Tim Griffith; **40–43** © Joe Fletcher; **44–49** © Eric Staudenmaier; **50–51** © Steve King; **52–53** © Paul Hester; **54–55** © Michael Vahrenwald; **56–59** © Will Crocker; **60–61** © PARA; **62 t** imageBROKER/Alamy Stock Photo; **62 b** Mykhailo Shcherbyna/Alamy Stock Photo; **63** vdbvsl/Alamy Stock Photo; **64** Andrew Cribb/Alamy Stock Photo; **65** Q-Images/Alamy Stock Photo; **66–67** © Mikiko Kikuyama; **68 tl** © Francesca Giovanelli; **68 tr** © Erik Freeland; **68b,** **69** © Raimund Koch; **70–73** © Lukas Wassmann/totalworld.com; **74** Charles Harker/Alamy Stock Photo; **76** © Inigo Bujedo Aguirre/VIEW; **79** © Werner Huthmacher/Artur/VIEW; **80** age fotostock/Alamy Stock Photo; **81** John Mitchell/Alamy Stock Photo; **82** John Coletti/Getty Images; **83** age fotostock/Alamy Stock Photo; **84–85** © Cristobal Palma; **86–89** © Cristobal Palma; **90** Paul Taylor/Alamy Stock Photo; **91** Aurelio Scetta/Alamy Stock Photo; **92** Diego Grandi/Alamy Stock Photo; **93** Xinhua/Alamy Stock Photo; **94–97** © Leonardo Finotti; **98–101** © Leonardo Finotti; **102–05** © Nelson Kon; **106–09** © Pezo von Ellrichshausen; **110–11** © Fernando Schapochnik; **112–15** © Fernando Schapochnik; **116–19** © Federico Cairoli; **120** frans lemmens/Alamy Stock Photo; **123** AC Manley/Alamy Stock Photo; **124** michael bracey/Alamy Stock Photo; **126–29** © Dinesen; **130** © Tuomas Uusheimo; **131** © Maija Luutonen; **132, 133** © Tuomas Uusheimo; **134–37** © Alice Clancy; **138** CW Images/Alamy Stock Photo; **139** Peter Horree/Alamy Stock Photo; **140** CAMimage/Alamy Stock Photo; **141** Londonstills.com/Alamy Stock Photo; **142, 143** © Mike Tsang; **144 t, 144 b** © Michael Sinclair; **145** © Mike Tsang; **146–47** © Dennis Gilbert/VIEW; **148–51** © Jack Hobhouse; **152–55** © Jack Hobhouse; **156** Hemis/Alamy Stock Photo; **157** B.O'Kane/Alamy Stock Photo; **158** Christian Müller/Alamy Stock Photo; **159** B.O'Kane/Alamy Stock Photo; **160–63** © Clément Guillaume; **164–67** © Roland Halbe; **168–71** © Hervé Abbadie; **172–75** © Ossip van Duivenbode; **176–79** © Tim Van de Velde; **180–81** © Peter Strobel; **182–85** © Rasmus Norlander; **186–89** © José Campos; **190–93** © Adrià Goula; **194–97** © Stefania Matteo, **198, 199 l, 199 r, 200** © George Messaritakis; **201 t, 201 b** © Yannis Drakoulidis; **202–05** Courtesy of Zaha Hadid Architects; **206** © courtesy of NLÉ; **208** Eric Lafforgue/Art in All of Us/Corbis via Getty Images; **211** jbdodane/Alamy Stock Photo; **212–13** Photo & architecture: Mathieu Hardy; **214–17** © Fernando Guerra; **218** © Alberto Heras; **219** © Javier Callejas; **220** Hemis/Alamy Stock Photo; **221** Peter Titmuss/Alamy Stock Photo; **222** imageBROKER/Alamy Stock Photo; **223** Thom Moore/Alamy Stock Photo; **224** © ETH Zurich U-TT/Daniel Schwartz; **225** © ETH Zurich U-TT; **226, 227 tl, 227 bl** © ETH Zurich U-TT/Dave Southwood; **227 r** © ETH Zurich U-TT/Daniel Schwartz; **228** © Michael Le Grange; **229, 230, 231** © Adam Letch; **232** eye35.pix/Alamy Stock Photo; **234** Sean Pavone/Alamy Stock Photo; **237** Chirag Wakaskar/Alamy Stock Photo; **238** Henry Westheim Photography/Alamy Stock Photo; **239** VisualAsia/Alamy Stock Photo; **240** eye35 stock/Alamy Stock Photo; **241** Hufton+Crow **242** © Linhan Zhang; **243** © Wang Ning; **244, 245 t, 245 b** © Xia Zhi; **246, 247 r** © ZAO/standardarchitecture; photographer: Wu Qingshan; **247 l** © ZAO/standardarchitecture; photographer: Wang Ziling; **248–51** © Edmon Leong; **252** Peter Schickert/Alamy Stock Photo; **253** Prasit Rodphan/Alamy Stock Photo; **254** © Collection Artedia/VIEW; **255** © Iwan Baan; **256–59** © In Keun Ryoo; **260–61** © Goong-sun Nam; **262–65** © Yongkwan Kim; **266** World Discovery/Alamy Stock Photo; **267** © Edmund Sumner/VIEW; **268** © Edmund Sumner/VIEW; **269** Bill Tingey/Arcaid Images; **270–73** © Kenichi Suzuki; **274 t** © Toshihiro Sobajima; **274 b, 275** © Jérémie Souteyrat; **276, 277** © Toshihiro Sobajima; **278–79** © Takuro Yamamoto Architects; **280, 281, 282** © Edmund Sumner; **283** © Matharoo Associates; **284–87** © Edmund Sumner; **288–91** © Eresh Weerasuriya; **292–97** © Wison Tungthunya; **298** Jean-Francois Périgois/Alamy Stock Photo; **299** Marla Holden/Alamy Stock Photo; **300** Rick Piper/Alamy Stock Photo; **301** HOANG DINH NAM/AFP/Getty Images; **302–05** © Hiroyuki Oki; **306–07** Hiroyuki Oki; **308–09** © Kent Soh; **310** Ulana Switucha/Alamy Stock Photo; **311** Thomas Cockrem/Alamy Stock Photo; **312** tustago/Alamy Stock Photo; **313** imageBROKER/Alamy Stock Photo; **314–15** © Derek Swalwell; **316–19** © Edward Hendricks; **320–23** © Mario Wibowo; **324** Paul Lovelace/Alamy Stock Photo; **327** Angela Wylie/The AGE/Fairfax Media via Getty Images; **328** Christine Wehrmeier/Alamy Stock Photo; **330** Fairfax Media/Fairfax Media via Getty Images; **331** imageBROKER/Alamy Stock Photo; **332** Robert Wallace/Wallace Media Network/Alamy Stock Photo; **333** © Richard Glover/VIEW; **334–35** © Peter Bennetts; **336–37** © Tom Ferguson; **338–41** © Peter Bennetts; **342–45** © Simon Devitt Photographer

On the front cover:
Telegraph Hill House, San Francisco, USA. See page 40.

On the back cover:
Vault House, Oxnard, USA. See page 44.

On page 2:
Views through levels and across different parts of the house allow for uninterrupted visual connections in Greja House, Singapore.

Published in association with
Yale University Press
P.O. Box 209040
New Haven, CT 06520-9040
yalebooks.com/art

This book was designed and produced by
White Lion Publishing
The Old Brewery
6 Blundell Street
London N7 9BH

Senior Editors	Carol King, Elspeth Beidas
Editor	Becky Gee
Designer	Josse Pickard
Picture Researcher	Laura Bulbeck
Editorial Assistant	Stacey Cleworth
Production Manager	Rohana Yusof
Editorial Director	Ruth Patrick
Publisher	Philip Cooper

Colour reproduction by Bright Arts
Printed in China
ISBN 978-0-300-23711-5
Library of Congress Control Number: 2018934784